Husband's Guide for the 21st Century

HG21C©

By M. Anthony Bell

HG21C © 2002
Copyright 2002 M. Anthony Bell, Sr.

© Copyright 2002 M. Anthony Bell. All rights reserved.

No part of this publication may be reproduced, stored in a retrieval system, or transmitted, in any form or by any means, electronic, mechanical, photocopying, recording, or otherwise, without the written prior permission of the author.

National Library of Canada Cataloguing in Publication Data

Bell, M. Anthony (Michael Anthony)
    HG21C : husband's guide for the 21th century / M. Anthony Bell.
    ISBN 1-55369-648-4
    1. Marriage. 2. Husbands--Conduct of life. I. Title.
HQ734.B49 2002   646.7'8   C2002-902722-5

TRAFFORD

This book was published *on-demand* in cooperation with Trafford Publishing.
On-demand publishing is a unique process and service of making a book available for retail sale to the public taking advantage of on-demand manufacturing and Internet marketing.
On-demand publishing includes promotions, retail sales, manufacturing, order fulfilment, accounting and collecting royalties on behalf of the author.

Suite 6E, 2333 Government St., Victoria, B.C. V8T 4P4, CANADA
Phone   250-383-6864   Toll-free   1-888-232-4444 (Canada & US)
Fax   250-383-6804   E-mail   sales@trafford.com
Web site   www.trafford.com   TRAFFORD PUBLISHING IS A DIVISION OF TRAFFORD HOLDINGS LTD.
Trafford Catalogue #02-0461   www.trafford.com/robots/02-0461.html

10   9   8   7   6   5   4   3   2

Author's Acknowledgements

To Valeria, my wife and best friend.
To my son, Tony - my motivator.

Sincere Thanks to the HG21C Focus Group

Anthony and Adel Pollard
Dr. Alan C. Peterson
Professor Marshalita Simms-Peterson
Charles Nwachukwu
Dr. Alvin Griffin
Fred and Dee Edmonson
Julia B. Schiebel
Steve and Hilma Jarrett
George and Jennifer (Pat) Thomas
Theresa Eldredge
Michael A. Jones
Wanda Murphy-Fulford
Dr. James Fason
Wesley and Raquel Clement
Brenda Warner
Les Brewer
David Breaden
Charles and Carolyn Rucker
Michael Bywalatz
and
To those who wish to remain Anonymous.

HG21C

The HG21C Cast

Cover and Illustrations were designed and produce by the
Author, utilizing AutoCadd 2000©
Copyright by AUTODESK, INC.

Special Thanks

Office Depot #137
Stone Mountain, Georgia

Print Department Staff

Mihib Mohamoud
Sagal Mohamed
And
Amed Sherif

For their outstanding customer service, patience and support during the editing of **HG21C** ©

TABLE OF CONTENTS

Introduction

A Note to Wives

Chapter One

Understand What's Between These Lines   1

Defining the Dilemma   4

The Power of the Movement   14

Making a Conscious Effort   25

Logical Thinking   32

Pleading Guilty   40

The Third Element   48

A Distant Third Place   52

Chapter Two

The Budget Officer   64

The Globetrotting Husband   68

Get a Girlfriend   76

Our Wife vs. Our Best Friend   78

Chapter Three

He's SO Sensitive   83

Household Chores and the Super Bowl   87

I'm Not Romantic Anymore?   90

The Toilet Seat and Dirty Underwear   94

Put Down Your Dukes... Honey   98

The Stepfather   103

Chapter Four

Commanding Respect   107

When Decisions become Regrets   113

The Stay-at-Home Dad   127

Christmas Parties and The Ride Home   131

Sacrificing Time   136

Our Wife's Best Friend   141

The Moon, the Stars, and a Rock   146

Final Note: To the Wives   168

HG21C

HG21C© 2002

Introduction

There are many realities that must be considered when we have the responsibility of being 21st Century Husbands (and fathers). After more than twenty years of marriage, I feel it's my duty and obligation to admit - we're in trouble.

HG21C is embarking into completely unfamiliar and uncharted territory. The "institution" of Husband-hood needs to be reviewed and overhauled in order to re-establish our noble positions.

After all, "never in history" have husbands had any reason to question what we should expect from our wives (?).

Many of us [husbands] *may* believe we have it all under control, However, if everything is "so" under control, - go to your wife right now and ask her, "Honey are you truly happy and satisfied with choosing me as your husband?" – Then be prepared for a moment of silence.

By all means, do not be disappointed if she hesitates. In fact, if she *does* answer the question, I will guarantee - she will then follow-up with the same question to you. So...

The "real" question is, "Will you be able to answer her question - honestly?"

HG21C has been written especially for the veteran husband, but will also assist the husband-to-be, and the newlywed.

The first few paragraphs *may* give one the impression that HG21C was written on how to be a better husband, - however, HG21C is really a guide on "how to make your wife - a better wife" and at the same time, a happier woman.

Calling all Vets

This is it. After five (or more) years of marriage, it's about time someone made some "sense" of it all. It's not that we're unhappy or dissatisfied, but rather confused.

One veteran husband asked,

"Why has this - so called, settled life, become so complicated?" And, "What happened to the girl

who, at one time, made me feel good about myself?"

Over the years, I searched for the answers, but all I found was information on "marriage or parenting" – [not husbanding].

I must admit - I panicked, had moments of dizzy spells - followed with periods of hiding in the basement or garage, pretending not to hear her calling my name. Sound familiar?

For many of us, we chose our mates for the mere reason "they made us feel good about ourselves". As selfish as this may sound, it's one of the few "wants" we [husbands] have. And another thing…

While most of us have embraced equal rights and opportunities for women in the workplace, the big question is, "How did "it" get in my house"?

Moreover, how do I express this feeling to my wife without challenging the *Movement?* Another question is, "What happened to us - after the kids were born?" And what happened to my favorite sneakers?

My interest in writing HG21C developed over the years purely because of my genuine affection for my wife and women in general. I will admit - my motivation has been based on pure selfishness. I wanted my wife to be a better wife.

We must admit - marital issues are one of the few topics we [husbands] discuss among ourselves. Even during my HG21C research, I found the typical [husbands] response to this topic was usually a passive shrug-of-the-shoulders.

Many veteran husbands (and wives) have contributed to the contents of HG21C. They have openly discussed their most sensitive issues while accepting the fact - my interest in this subject is completely sincere and worthy of discussion.

By reading HG21C, you will be able to completely *Define the Dilemma* and more importantly, learn the strategies which will empower you to get her to gladly respond to you, without [you hearing] her annoying response "What about me"?

Please note - the majority of HG21C was written in "first person". The terms "us, our, and we" were chosen for the simplicity of allowing "you" to understand - "we" are in this challenge together – against the status quo.

Warning: Any attempt to practice the strategies discussed in HG21C – without completion, is NOT recommended.

Newlywed or Husband to-be

If you are the newlywed or husband-to-be, you will probably benefit most from HG21C - for the mere reason - you can preview the coming attractions.

Hopefully, the woman you have chosen has the ability to inspire you to be a better man by realizing and nurturing your potential. And in turn – you take every advantage by supporting her goals and aspirations - in the home as well as in her career goals.

The Moon, the Stars, and a Rock was written with the newlywed/husband-to-be in mind. I am certain you will instantly be amused by this enlightening metaphor.

…I remember, like it was yesterday, when I asked myself if "settling down" was the best decision for me (?). And although - being single has its benefits, there comes a time when we must put our toys away and think about the future. However, before you are allowed to venture into HG21C, there are a few issues we must discuss:

No. 1 – You know those back and shoulder rubs your fiancé "eagerly" gives you, without asking?

No. 2 – You know how she laughs and/or giggles at all those silly things you say?

No. 3 – You know how - when you are driving, she sits there and does not question your driving skills?

No. 4 – You know how she doesn't say much when you decide to play 18 holes and then stop off for a couple of beers?

…never mind.

Note to the Wives:

My wife is like most of you, - a mother, has professional obligations and also has the instinctive dedication to be the facilitator of the household. In other words, (for some of you) "Coming home can *sometimes* be a complete horror".

When I actually considered all of your responsibilities, I had to ask myself, "How can anyone expect her to [also] be attentive to my selfish "wants"?

I also noted - after a typical day at the office, we would both come home having the same needs. - Someone waiting at home to appreciate and pamper us. Thus, we have become the same creatures of "wants and needs".

I am certain most of you wish you had the energy to be completely attentive to your husbands. - Or perhaps, for some of you, it is not your lack of energy, but more - your lack of motivation (?).

However, your lack of motivation is not intentional. The status quo has simply put too much on your plate of responsibilities. In addition, you have been conditioned, over the last generation or so - to proudly represent the *Movement.*

Please understand - HG21C does not challenge the [Women's] *Movement* - directly, but rather explains how "it" has indirectly affected the balance of the husband and wife relationship at home. Somehow we must be able to distinguish the husband/wife relationship from the male/female relationship in a general sense.

HG21C attempts to explain to husbands, the positive and negative elements that influence our lives from a husband's point of view. HG21C also attempts to suggest to husbands many fair and logical approaches to neutralize almost any situation with regard to the husband/wife relationship.

By comparison, wives have had the comfort of discussing family and marital concerns among yourselves. Husbands however, have not been conditioned to express our selves, (to ourselves) when it comes to similar marital matters.

So, if you found HG21C hidden under his car seat, in the basement or tool shed, please understand we love you dearly and are making a valiant effort to make you happier than you have ever been – as a wife. We sincerely ask that you trust us in this endeavor.

While HG21C has been written with your husband in mind, you may find - you cannot resist. If this is the case, I hope you will find HG21C to be enlightening and entertaining.

Furthermore, in the event your flannel PJ's have suddenly disappeared – without a trace, please accept my sincere apology.

Again, we love you.

CHAPTER 1

UNDERSTAND WHAT'S BETWEEN THESE LINES

When we say, "Thank you" to someone, why do we then expect him or her to follow with "You're welcome"? After all, we're thanking "them" for some sort of courtesy or favor. - Right?

I'm guessing - if the person "really" wanted to do the favor, or the favor was not a bother, saying - "You're welcome", would be one way they could "genuinely" express - they did not mind doing the favor. So…

How do we feel when a person does not say, "You're welcome"? Do we then *question* whether they actually "wanted" to do the favor?

Some courtesies have just become customary in our everyday communication with people.

When greeting women for example, notice we usually - make eye contact, then a little smile? And when the woman is a good distance away, we'll add a wave. But not a regular wave, we wave - not with just our hands, but more with our fingers. After all, it's a girl.

Think about it, when was the last time we greeted a woman with a nod? Or for that fact, when was the last time we waved at another man - with our fingers, followed with a smile?

Because of our genuine affection for women and especially our wives, we are blessed with the natural instincts to react to their feminine charms. And the "way" they choose to return the greeting, could inspire us to be charming or more affectionate as well. Moreover, it sets the tone on the type of relationship we have, or want to have.

After being married for more than a few years, it's understandable how we lose the "motivation" to be charming and affectionate towards our wives. One of the ways we can tell if we are "guilty" is to ask ourselves, "How often do I make my wife smile, laugh or giggle"?

Let us also remind ourselves of the time when we dedicated "all we did" to impress the woman that eventually became our wife. - Remember when she would laugh or giggle at nearly everything we said, and how it made us feel?

During that time, she was also motivated to appreciate our "manly charms". The reason she responded that way was not accidental, but rather, "we" invested a great deal of time and effort in making her giggle. Also during those days, her reaction to our favors made us feel good about ourselves – and she knew it.

This problem is fairly universal in most marriages. We [husbands] become complacent and believe "this is the way life is going to be". Meanwhile, she has the opinion - we have become less romantic, boring and worst of all - predictable.

As we immediately refer to *Defining the Dilemma*, we can understand why she "rarely displays the charming character" - that once made us feel good about ourselves. And while we *could* blame her for not making the effort (to react to our "manly charms"), we must approach this problem as if – "Husbands are the only one's who can correct the *Dilemma*".

TO BE CONTINUED.

DEFINING THE DILEMMA

After a day at the office, our fathers and grandfathers walked through the door of their homes. Waiting for him was someone that was completely dedicated to his comfort and happiness – his wife. She was also responsible for maintaining the home and nurturing the kids – all by herself.

That's right, most of our moms were very good at their responsibilities as wives. In fact, it seemed as if our moms catered to dad's comfort, more so - than she did the kids. Meanwhile, a husband's household responsibility was to "manage his empire".

Today it's different – to say the least. Today, to even speak of the topic mentioned in the last two paragraphs "publicly" would set off civil unrest, followed by an emergency meeting of the City Council.

Before we can prescribe a solution to *our* dilemma, it must first be "defined". But how do we put our concerns into words without appearing as if we are complaining that our wives are not doing enough – as wives?

As was mentioned in the *Introduction,* HG21C is embarking into "completely uncharted territory". We must admit - we have an issue or two that needs to be brought out into the open, or at least discussed among ourselves.

Never in history have husbands had any reason to question what we should expect from our wives (?). We must also admit that due to *The Power of the Movement,* the odds are completely against us from a societal standpoint. One good example is to note "how" the term *wife* is defined by the most recognized and respected source – the dictionary.

I strongly suggest - you sit down for this one…

Popular dictionaries define a *wife* as simply "a married woman" or "the spouse of a man". That's it (?). - No references or definitions of her responsibilities to the husband?

My first thought was - "Darn!"

It is important we agree - this information does absolutely nothing for those of us who are searching for answers. Sadly, the dictionary was supposed to be our friend and help us in time of need, – but nooo.

During my research, I asked many wives "how would [she] define the definition or responsibilities of a *wife (?)*. Their answers were startling. Most wives seemed to accept and even appreciate - they have no real "defined responsibility (D R)" to their husbands.

All together now - "Damn!"

And what's worse, - "We didn't get the Memo".

Had we known five (or more) years ago, that no "D R" had been established; we would have requested some sort of warranty, or at least an operator's manual. It then became clear, - somehow, *they* failed to forward us [husbands] a copy of the "The Memo". - And for the sake of "the future of Husband-hood", - HG21C was dedicated and determined to find it.

The search took me down many dark alleys, - to meet with "shadowing figures" - standing in abandoned doorways. There were also those who denied the existence of any such Memo, - just to throw me off track. Then it happened. HG21C finally uncovered "The Memo" - old and yellowed with brittle edges. It seemed to have been written in a strange language, which required many hours of translation by renowned scholars.

HG21C / 7

HG21C© 2002

8 / HG21C

Some of these terms – to this day, have yet to be translated.

MEMORANDUM

Date: January 21, 1992

To: Movement Supporters
From: Movement HQ, Definition Division
Re: Description Modification – wife

Hear yea, hear yea,

Due to the Movement's Agenda referenced, the Board shall study the resolution to form a Special Committee to activate and appoint the Chief Directive to redefine the definition of the term *wife*. So the Board states - "hither-with".

All previous definitions or references to any terms or descriptions associated with the term *"wife"* have been dissolved. So the Board recommends - " *now-ith*".

Any future definitions referenced to "that word" will be defined as the Board agrees. As the Directive dictates, all parties formerly associated with that term, shall be referred to as "W*omen*" – *"now-ith with us-ith"*.

Menwhile, and "forth com-ith", the Board has directed to elect a Special Committee to oversee the Strategy Forum to study the elimination of any word or term associated as "opposite" of the term to be dissolved. So the Board recommends, as so approved - "hither-with-a-gin-ith".

N.O.W. - Go do-ith now-ith

One could argue - wives who work outside the home are justified in their position on limiting the attention they offer to their husbands. However, even the wives that *could* "stay at home" and nurture the home and dedicate attention to their husbands (and children), would prefer to expend a great portion of their energies "outside the home".

In other words, if we were to ask [wives] who are presently working "outside the home", whether she would prefer to "stay at home"(?), she would, in most cases, *say* "Yes", but would eventually become bored and insist to have more responsibilities outside the home.

We cannot "completely" understand why our wives would rather expend a great portion of their energies outside the home. - And to ponder on the present state of her intentions would be "a waste of our time". So, let's make it simple by accepting the following:

Women of today and especially our wives, have more to offer. They are more intelligent, better educated and have the motivation to be more productive (outside the home) than their predecessors. Bless their hearts.

However, it seems as if, - over the past twenty years or so, as we [husbands] embraced equal rights and opportunities for women in the workplace, we [husbands] failed to read the "fine print".

Hoodwinked or Sacrificed?

While the *Movement* has made tremendous strides, it has also "interrupted" the basic foundation of our society – home and family. After all, "something" had to be sacrificed.

The fact is - we sincerely appreciate the opportunities, which are now available to our sisters, daughters and wives. The most direct impact on the family is - in many of today's households, a wife can easily earn as much, or more salary than her husband.

This is significant and has contributed greatly to our demand for larger homes, second cars and many other "luxuries" which would otherwise not have been attainable.

On the other hand, women of today, and especially our wives, seem to struggle with "letting their hair down", after five o'clock. Thus, their inability to become "feminine in nature" (and their lack of "giggling"), aids in establishing the dilemma.

This self-proclaimed "D R" of the role of a "wife" has created a question or two (??). Questions like - "Who is responsible for managing the home"? And if "Who manages" the home *is* the question, "What's the answer"?

As we ponder the notion – "it's simply a question of management", we must be certain that "studying the notion" is worthy of our time and consideration. After all, managing our Empires in the 21st Century will not be an easy task.

HG21C research has found - the responsibility of managing the home is more a by-product of *Commanding Respect*. And if the position of "household manager" is what we [husbands] want…I am certain our wives will gladly grant us her permission (?).

Thus, we must continue our quest for the "true question".

After many years of researching for the "true question", I finally acquired the "guts" to approach our *Dilemma* selfishly.

"What do We [husbands] Want"?

For many of us, when we are faced with this question, we lose the ability to speak and become completely dumbfounded. And as the question is being asked, we can tell by the look in *her* eyes, that our answer had better be complete and most of all - justified.

However, one would think - after more than a few years of marriage, our wives would have some idea of what we "want" - as oppose to what we "need" (?).

Truthfully, I believe she can distinguish the difference. After all – she's intelligent (?). But for some strange reason, she feels completely justified in requiring - we submit our request in triplicate and through the proper channels.

Thus, making our dilemma more complicated than it needs to be.

HG21C Sidebar:

As the reader, I can imagine what is going through your minds right now, but we must go forward. It is also important that we do not panic at this point. Additionally, HG21C strongly suggest - if your heart is beating louder than usual, or you are experiencing a little dizziness, perhaps you should take a break. If not, you will probably need to reread the last three paragraphs before continuing.

The Answer

(Quietly) All we want - is for our wives to concentrate on being "wifely", by meeting "our" expectations as their husbands. (Louder) All right, now that we have said it out loud, how do we now - define "wifely"?

Saying and Doing

Our biggest challenge is "how" do we tell our wives we want them to "attend" to us by "saying and doing things" that make us feel good about ourselves, - the way she did before the kids. (?)

Furthermore, when we attempt to sincerely express ourselves, it sounds to her as if we are stating, "she is not doing enough".

The only way our soul mates can truly understand us, is to accept the fact - we have a valid concern. Thus we are justified.

We could start by questioning whether or not she has the energy or motivation to make a conscious attempt (?). But whatever we do, we cannot ask these questions out loud, but rather - be satisfied that "she should" have the energy and motivation.

In addition to convincing her that being a loving and attentive wife requires *Making a Conscious Effort* on her part, we must also convince her that making the effort does not conflict with the *Movement's* agenda. Moreover, she made the promise - in front of God and a few hundred witnesses.

<u>The Bottom Line</u>

"Yes", we [husbands] have mostly been hoodwinked. And as we assess the damage, we have two choices. We can either:

1) Sit back and lick our wounds, as discussed in *Victims of the Movement,* or

2) Take the honorable approach by accepting defeat in the battle and to regroup to win the war.

Accept it, not as a problem, but as a challenge to a worthy adversary.

THE POWER OF THE MOVEMENT

As husbands, the biggest challenge we face is the [Women's] *Movement*. In fact, the *Movement* is the reason most wives believe - equal status in the household is their "right". However, what she chooses to define as her "right" - should correctly be defined as a "privilege".

While wives have always had this privilege, their "right" causes them to "abuse the privilege". The abuse usually occurs, (when they regard "shopping" as therapy) or especially, when they make us (or situations) more complicated than they really are. The fact is - we're simple.

Today, our primary responsibilities at home are not much different than our wives. We can safely admit -besides the "husband/wife" titles, we have pretty much evolved requiring the same "wants/needs" - respectively. We have to also admit - it has become pretty darn confusing.

It has gotten to the point, where we [husbands] have no idea what to expect when we get home after a hard days work, because she's coming home from a hard days work as well. Thus, we are both expecting to be greeted by someone who

appreciates our efforts, – someone like a wife. But where is she?

HG21C has found - the reason we seldom experience being "tended to", is indirectly caused by our wives obligation to the *Movement*. And no matter how we question her lack of motivation of being "wifely", we are either accused of being typical men or "insensitive to her needs".

So…the big question is, "Do we have what it takes to get her back?"

It's easy to accept her positioning if we understand the "power and influence" of the *Movement*.

Heathcliff: Last of the Great TV Husbands

Look around and take note of "how" we [husbands] are generally portrayed. Television alone portrays *most* husbands as being - immature, lazy, wife-beaters, and bigamist - irresponsible or just plain silly.

Back in the mid-1980's, for example, our favorite show on television was "The Cosby Show". Not just for the humor and entertainment, but it also aided in [husbands] our ability to appreciate and support our career-minded wives – similar to the very charming and "wifely" - Claire. Little did we realize - it was just the beginning of our downfall (?).

As we look back over the years, with regard to the negative portrayal of husbands [men] on television and other mediums, we must consider how those influences *could* affect the way women generally regard men. Thus, it could be safe to assume that 21st century women have adopted an adversarial opinion of men.

HG21C Sidebar:

Please do not misunderstand my inference. The fact is - most of us [men and women] are gullible when it comes to "what" influences our opinions of *some* people.

An example would be how some ethnic groups have been portrayed in history books, on television or other mediums. - Which is how many people have been programmed to believe and accept negative stereotypes of *some* people.

Women's magazines have been the source of my attempts to understand the "evolution of women" for many years. I can recall articles from as far back as the 1980's, which suggested to women to be "independent", or to "not depend on a man". So...

The next time we are sitting in the waiting room of our dentist or physician's office, let's pick up the copy of Cosmo or Essence, instead of Sports Illustrated. Don't be embarrassed, it's the only way we can get a "bit of insight" on how women have been influenced over the years.

Acknowledging the Movement

It is my opinion - many of these [magazine] articles along with television, - have created a generation (or two) of women who have never really acquired the understanding of how their feminine nature and charm is a "powerful motivator" to men. REPEAT

In other words, they [women] have been programmed (if you will) into being "adversarial in nature" - for the sake of the *Movement*.

Don't get me wrong, equal rights and opportunity for women, in the "workplace" are indeed a good thing. However, over the years, the *Movement* has derailed and has created many unpleasant challenges for those of us who have chosen to settle down and become husbands (and fathers).

Many of these challenges are apparent when we look to our wives to be supportive in our decisions as being the head of the household.

Pardon me.

The fact is, due to political correctness, even the term "head of the household" is a *questionable* term. Moreover, today's women believe "men of today" are completely responsible for the disenfranchisement of women - in the past. By comparison, it's similar to blaming "today's majority community" as being responsible for the discrimination of minorities in the past.

Please pardon the analogy, but the seriousness of our dilemma *is* a societal problem. Moreover, when it comes to "how women" *could* regard their husbands today, we can safely assume the worse. Only then - can we [husbands] understand how our wives *could* question our intentions to be honorable and loving husbands. One husband states;

My own challenge over the years has been to convince my wife that it is not fair or feasible for her to believe that "I" represent "men" in general.

The Bottom line:

We [husbands] have been misrepresented by the status quo, by being placed in the general category of men. This misrepresentation has negatively affected the way - our wives, children and society regard our once honorable position.

Victims of the Movement

There are many husbands having a rough time. He wonders around aimlessly searching for Truth, Justice and the remote control. The victims also believe that "being cooperative" - by always "agreeing with her" is the politically correct way to be.

However, little does he realize, - his wife is just waiting for him to show - at least, a little backbone.

Wives' like Loraine…

We all have a neighbor like Pete. He's the guy that can "never come out and play". He seemed like a great guy in the beginning.

Pete was always working in the yard, edging the lawn and trimming the hedges. But as the years have gone by, I noticed - Pete can't leave the yard, let alone - take a ride to Home Depot.

In the past, we have invited Pete and his wife Loraine to our home, but they always seemed to have a last minute emergency.

On one occasion, Pete and I had planned to get up early Saturday and take a ride to Home Depot. Pete needed to replace 50 feet of garden hose for watering the lawn. I was just going along for the male bonding and maybe check out the riding lawn mowers.

That morning, I rang their doorbell. Surprisingly, Loraine answered the door and immediately said, "Pete is busy" and would call me later. Disappointed, I asked if Pete needed any help or could I pick up the water hose for him (?). She slowly closed the door while stating again, that Pete would call me later.

For a moment, I thought "I" was the idiot, - then it hit me. – Pete is a victim of the Movement.

The reason Pete spends so much time in the yard is to get out of the house and as far away from Loraine as he can get. I also guessed that the new water hose would have given him greater distance.

HG21C / 23

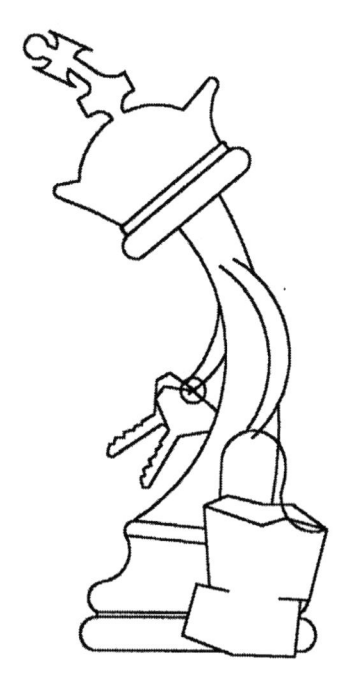

Now when I see Pete, standing there watering the lawn - with a 25 foot water hose, re-enforced with duct tape, I feel sorry for him. He waves, while attempting to present a "neighborly" smile. But he looks more like a man with severe abdominal pains.

The "victims" are also seen in the malls and department stores. He stands there, while his wife is in the dressing room, - holding his car keys in one hand and her purse in the other. His posture is that of an 80-year-old man, sagging shoulders and no backbone. He stands there sporting the "outfit" his wife purchased "On Sale". Occasionally, he will look our way – as if to reach out for salvation, or for someone to save him from the forces that stole his spirit. It's a pitiful sight. Another brother bites the dust.

Not to sound melodramatic, but there are many of our brothers out there suffering. As unfortunate as it is - for many husbands, it's too late. And as selfish as this may sound, we must step over them, we have our own agendas. We can only help those [husbands] who want to help themselves. So when we see Pete and other victims like him, we must be certain they are worthy of our time and consideration, - before we slip them a copy of HG21C.

MAKING A CONSCIOUS EFFORT

Imagine if being married required an annual evaluation - much like we have at the office.

We are notified in advance, when our performance evaluation will be, and with self-discipline and dedication to our professional obligations, we prepare.

Again imagine, after five or ten years of marriage, our wife announces - *our* evaluation is scheduled for next week. She will also give us the opportunity to "self-evaluate" ourselves, in which we will both review - next week during our performance evaluation.

While some of us may challenge the notion of "marriage evaluations", it's truly worthy of our consideration. After all, how else could we gauge our performance – as husbands? And if we were to take the matter seriously, by whose standards would be considered valid (?).

HG21C Sidebar:

Before we begin to acknowledge "standards", let us refer to the definition of the term - *husband*.

Hus-band (hŭz′bend) *n.* **1.** *abbr.* h., H. a man joined to a women in marriage; a women's spouse. **2.** *Archaic.* A manager or steward, as of a household or wine cellar. **3.** A prudent and thrifty manager, as of money or expenses. *– tr. v.* **husbanded, -banding, -dands. 1.** To spend or use economically; to budget; to conserve: *husband one's energy.* **2.** *Rare,* To marry. **3.** *Archaic.* To find a husband for. [Middle English *housbonde, hus (e) bonde,* husband, husbandman, Old English *hūsbonda,* master of a household, husband, from Old Norse *hūsbōndi: hūs,* house, from Germanic *hūsam (unattested),* HOUSE + bōndi, earlier *bōandi, būandi.* Present participal of *bōa, būa,* to dwell (see **bheu-** in Appendix*.]

The American Heritage Dictionary of the English Language, 1978, by Houghton Mifflin Company. Page 643.

Before we get too excited and organize an Annual Husband's Convention or go running to our wives to show them our newly found existence, it would be to our advantage to keep this information to ourselves. In fact, I highly recommend - we regard this information as TOP SECRET.

During my research, I presented this "definition of husband" to many of the wives, while insisting that she "read it out loud". Their reactions became surprisingly predictable, - whereas, most interjected the term "bullsh*t" into the definition (?).

As they interjected "that term", it was amazing how "my" dictionary seemed to magically leave their hands and fly across the room.

After seeing "my" dictionary endure many unsuccessful flights, I learned that it would be prudent to ask them to read the definition from their own dictionary.

As we pick-up on the topic of our wives standards or definition of the term *husband,* we must be careful "not" to combine her definition with the dictionary's definition – unless we have many years of handling "nitro and glycerin" - BOOM.

Her Standards, period

Realistically, from the moment we said, "I do", it has been our responsibility to be "whatever" our wife, reasonably expects of us. In fact, we also promised to do so - in front of God and a couple of hundred witnesses.

Dedicating ourselves to the happiness and well being of our wives is an honorable effort and should be placed in the highest regard. Even if we have kids, our wife should still be the first and foremost priority in our lives.

While most of us have always placed our wives in the highest regard, - the question is, "Are we giving her what she needs, or expects"?

For the record, it is important that we do not complicate matters by attempting to compare our "wants" to her "needs". Simply, "women have needs", period.

The Handwriting on the Wall

There are many indirect consequences that could occur if we fail to completely accept the "notion" of her required needs. And for many of us, we will not experience the consequences until it's too late.

With this said, let's pretend as if we found this letter in our mailbox one day.

To the husband of my co-worker,

Every morning I wait to see her walk through the main entrance of our office. I try not to appear too excited, after all, I see her everyday.

We have become fairly close over the last few months. There have been times when I felt - the little bit of attention that I gave her while working, usually made her day.

I must also admit - your wife is truly an adorable woman, and has a cute twinkle in her eyes when she giggles or laughs out loud. I have always been attracted to her, but kept a distance because she was married with children.

Our relationship was strictly professional until one day I noticed she did not have that special glow. - I am sure you remember that "glow" (?).

As the afternoon passed, I noticed her glancing in my direction as she worked. At the end of the day, she asked if I could hang around after work and walk her to the car.

As we walked to the parking deck, I was careful not to say much - knowing something serious was on her mind. To perk her up, I thought she would enjoy talking about your kids. She said that they were fine, and again went silent.

As we approached her car, she stopped, dropped her purse, fell to her knees and broke down in tears. In a crying stammer, she said, "I don't want to go home".

I was completely dumbfounded. She asked me to take her somewhere where we could talk. She gave me her keys – I opened the passenger door and helped her to the seat. As we sat, I reached for her hand to comfort her. She then leaned to rest her head on my shoulder.

After a few moments, she said, "Since the kids were born, you have failed to express any kind of affection towards her, and that going home has become a horror". END

It's not important how this story ended. But if you must know, he did not take advantage of her emotional state - he was a gentleman and a friend.

What we must ask is, – What is it that makes it so convenient for wives to assume that husbands are the responsible party?

We could again, fault the *Movement* in this regard, however, we must also admit that over time, it has become somewhat of a challenge for us [husbands] to express our love and affection to our wives, - (the way we use to) but why?

It's quite easy to understand how *some* of us have given up, and perhaps wished she would seek affection elsewhere, or rather [we] express our love and affection to someone else. If these thoughts have entered your mind, put them on hold for now as we refer to *When Decisions become Regrets.*

The Bottom line:

It seems as if many "wives" have chosen to position themselves as "women" - in a general sense. Furthermore, it's unfortunate – the lovely woman we call our wife, has unknowingly become an agent for the opposition.

Don't get me wrong, her "subversive acts" are not intentional. She has accepted the notion that "representing the *Movement*" is a full-time responsibility, which conflicts with the idea of being "wifely".

On the other hand, if we fail to make a "conscious effort" by expressing an interest in "what's important to her" - there's always another man that will. And we can imagine what his motivation is.

LOGICAL THINKING

Log-ic [noun] *1) the study of the principles of reasoning. 2) The relationship of element to element to whole in a set of objects, individuals, principles or events.*

Basically, *logic* is black or white (no grays), right or wrong. We must use logic in our approach to a simple task or to the ultimate challenge. In any case, it's how we "choose" to approach a specific challenge or task.

It is my opinion that 5-year-old kids are basically more *logical* than high school seniors. This could perhaps be due to the theoretical (or rational) approach to teaching, as employed by our educational institutions. Here's a familiar example:

A glass filled half way with water.

Is the glass, half full or half empty?

Many believe an argument can be made that the glass is half "empty", - by attempting to employ a rational approach to the question. We could agree with this concept if the subject were math or science. But there is absolutely no such thing as being "half" of empty.

Thus, the "logical" answer is half full. Period.

During the editing of HG21C, a member the "focus group" challenged the logical answer. This is what she said,

"If the glass was empty, and you filled it half way, then it's half full". She added, *"If it was filled to the top, and half was drunk, then it's half empty".*

- Bless her heart. (Making it more complicated than it really is.)

<u>Einstein Speaks</u>

Let's admit it guys, one of our biggest problems (while responding to our wives) is "not thinking before we speak". We say stupid things all the time, because we do not take a moment (or two) to formulate an intelligent thought.

Logical thinking is the foundation of genius.
– Einstein.

Without beating around the bush, let's consider a few "basic life" questions:

1) Of all the elements in our lives, what are absolutely the most important?

2) At what stage in our lives can we claim to be a success? And,
3) At what age do we actually begin to "think of our words", before we speak them out loud?

Many of our decisions as husbands and in life, can be made quite easy by accepting these "top three" questions - as priorities.

HG21C Sidebar:

As we prepared for our forever-changing society, we must all seek the motivation to keep up. Keeping up with technology, for example, is indeed required in order to ensure employment and of course - eating. – But of course, we knew *that*.

Our motivation in this area is basically career driven and $$$. And for those of us who have accepted this fact, we have accepted it - because it's "just plain logical". So…

Why is it "not logical" to keep up with - how the family unit - has, and continues to evolve?

Approaching Her "Moments" - Logically

Generally, when any person acts or reacts in a questionable manner, no matter how unreasonable or ridiculous their position, there is "always a logical" and acceptable reason as to "why".
REPEAT

When it comes to our wives, all we need to know is "who or what" is influencing them. Only then, can we approach the issue logically.

Acknowledging the influence - will not only allow us to understand and accept her attitude or position, but it will also provide us with the essential tools to reasonably approach the *Dilemma*. All we need to know is - "What" to say or do, and "When" to say or do.

This approach can come in handy when our wives say or do "anything" that causes us to respond by utilizing our "high-toned vocal cords". It is amazing how they have the ability to make us react to *some* questions or situations as if *we* are complete idiots.

One mistake we make as husbands is to feel an obligation to "immediately respond" to a question, - no matter how ridiculous the question. And when one asks a ridiculous question – without thinking, chances are, - the answer "will" be just as ridiculous. - Unless we [husbands] take the time to "think" about our response - first.

Logically, the best way to respond to a ridiculous question is to calmly "repeat the question". Thus, allowing the troublemaker to "think" and perhaps, reconsider *her* position. On the other hand, to minimize putting ourselves in these "questionable" positions, we should focus on *Commanding Respect.*

Gauging Success

Many of us 'believe" we are keeping up - as husbands. But are we really?

Our families "are" the most important elements in our lives, are they not? Could we then assume - our "success in life" has a great deal to do with the way we prioritize our responsibilities as husbands (and fathers)?

Our success also depends on not becoming misguided or influenced by the *elements,* which threaten our ability to feel like "real men".

Salary vs. The Hero

Though many of us are earning a salary that exceeds our wife's income, we cannot be certain "the income advantage" is all that is required to satisfy our responsibilities as a husband. In fact, adding this "advantage" to the equation probably places the "six-figure husband" - for example, in a worse position than his middle-class counterpart. - Simply because of his lack of motivation to *Make a Conscious Effort* to a wife who "needs" more than just financial security.

On the other hand, suppose our wife earns a bit more $$$. - Are we embarrassed? Do we feel less of a man?

If [you] fall into this category, get over it! Or perhaps get a part-time job to supplement your salary. – *If* you believe - making more $$$ will make you "manly" in the eyes of your wife.

Realistically, from her point of view, earning a higher salary is no big deal. What's most important to her - is for [you] us to be her "hero".

Being a hero for our wives does not mean, "Leaping tall buildings in a single bound", but rather - has more to do with the little things.

Allowing another man, for example, to be our wife's hero can not only be embarrassing, but in some cases - disastrous.

Therefore, at the top of our list - *could* be that we "learn to fix things". I am not suggesting we take a HVAC night course at the community college or put on a cape with a red "S". What I'm suggesting is, take command of what needs to be fixed, adjusted, replaced or blown up.

HG21C cannot express enough - the importance of being "in charge" of the safety and comfort of our Empires.

Do-it Yourself-ith

For instance, there are basically 4 major systems in our homes. They include the electrical, plumbing, heat/air and "her car". The electrical is pretty much a system that will take care of itself, but "her car will not". So make sure she has the newer, more dependable vehicle.

The plumbing *could* give us a bit of concern on occasion. - Then there's the HVAC. Just go by your favorite home improvement center, pick up a "How To Guide on Whatever", and don't be afraid to put on a tool belt.

Speaking of plumbing problems:

Roger and Lynn bought a three-bedroom home in the northern suburbs. The home was basically in good shape, except for one of the faucets in the bathroom. But, because there were two sinks in the bathroom, repairing the broken faucet was not a priority for Roger to replace.

After years of living with one sink, Lynn's dad visited and noted one of the faucets needed replacing. Lynn's dad immediately took control of the situation. He went out - purchased and installed the faucet, all in less than two hours.

While Lynn's dad did what any father would have done for his baby-girl, I am certain he had no intention of making Roger look like an idiot – to put it mildly.

The Bottom Line:

As the story suggested, Lynn's dad "took control" - period. Meanwhile, Roger - not only earns less salary than Lynn, but is also standing there looking like an idiot, while wondering why his father-in-law never allows him to light the gas grill.

PLEADING GUILTY

On occasion, we [husbands] can be "guilty" of being completely innocent.

When it comes to communicating with our wives, we must remember - one of the reasons we married her was because she is intelligent. Thus, we are obligated to respond to her with a certain degree of intelligence and respect. After all, if anyone deserves these courtesies, it's our wives.

Admitting our mistakes is truly an honorable position for us to take in most cases.

<u>Order in the Kingdom</u>

As a general rule, we are indeed responsible to neutralize any *element* that interrupts the harmony of our households – no matter what. REPEAT

Accepting this responsibility is the only way we can successfully lay the foundation of trust and fairness as we manage our tiny Empires.

During my research, I asked a few veteran husbands to share their wisdom and experience. Here's a story from a twelve-year veteran husband.

One evening after speaking to a female co-worker on the phone about some work related issue, my wife stated, "she knew" I was speaking to a "woman" by the tone of my voice.

She immediately followed with the question, "How come you don't speak to "me" with the same "sultry tone"?

"What are you taking about"? Was my first thought, but I didn't say it.

Thinking…

Instead, I accepted her question as legitimate and responded, "I don't know honey, let's think about it".

More thinking…

I realized - it would have been an insult to my wife's intelligence had I denied her assertion. So…

While answering my wife's question, I explained the reason "I believe" I speak to other women in "that" way, is perhaps, "because of the way they respond [to me]".

In other words - Honey, "Other women tend to be more accepting, charming, and not so quick to challenge or criticize".

Again, she asked "why", and I explained what I "believed" to be the reason. My answer was truthful, and gave my wife something to think about. END

Man… he's good. (He should write a book.).

On the other hand, we must consider the "reasons" why some of our female acquaintances respond to us in ways, which causes us to modify our tone of voice by appearing to be "more charming", compared to how we generally communicate with our wives.

Moments like these can usually inspire our wives to question our intentions or suggest - *I'm Not Romantic Anymore?*

<u>The Bottom line:</u>

No matter how strong or confident our wives appear to be, we must accept the fact - the foundation of her happiness is usually based on fulfilling her emotional "needs". Thus, they have a need to be constantly reassured that her concerns and interests are important to us - as discussed in *He's SO Sensitive*.

Understanding it is our responsibility to "tend" to her emotional needs - is "essential to a husbands happiness". REPEAT.

Whether the issues are family, work, or play, they should all be approached with adequate thought and logic.

Who's at Fault?

Quite simply, we are never *intentionally* wrong. - We may be guilty of "not thinking", but again, never wrong.

After being married for more than a year or two, you're probably wondering, "What happened?" It can seem as if we are accused of "not doing", more often than doing.

We all remember the early days when she would accept our shortcomings - such as our memory lapses or our inability to pay attention.

Now she expects us to defend something we said or did - six months before we were married. We can also find ourselves victims of bad timing.

Here's a familiar scenario.

At the end of the work day;

Leslie is the first to arrive home - it's quiet. No one's calling Leslie's name, "ah", the workday is over. - Leslie is blessed with about thirty minutes to "chill".

Meanwhile, Jackie is still in rush-hour traffic...

Jackie finally arrives thirty minutes later.

From the moment Jackie walks through the door, Leslie "attacks" Jackie with question after question about their day.

The "tone" of Jackie's response is not acceptable to Leslie.

Leslie then asked Jackie, "WHAT'S WRONG WITH YOU"?

Jackie immediately snaps back, " What's wrong with ME? WHAT'S WRONG WITH YOU"?

Thus, an argument is in the making.

Most couples have had this experience. In fact, many couples don't even make it beyond this point.

This scenario could have been avoided if Jackie had scheduled some "chill time" before walking through the door. After all, Jackie has experienced the same type of "greeting" from Leslie many times in the past.

So what could Jackie have done to avoid this type of scenario? - Jackie could have remained in the car long enough to listen to a favorite CD – twice, or by pretending to listen to the news, before facing the "relaxed" Leslie.

The Trouble Maker

Leslie was indeed responsible for this prelude to war. Leslie failed by having higher expectations than Jackie could deliver at that particular time. In other words, bad timing. In this case, Leslie should have merely greeted Jackie with a kiss.

The "Leslie/Jackie" analogy was chosen because gender is not the issue and does not prejudice us into thinking which of us (husband/wife) is responsible. What's most important is - which of us will accept the responsibility of taking action to avoid these kinds of situations in the future (?).

Damned if I do, Damned if I Don't

We must learn to laugh-it-off or go completely insane – or jail. After many years of marriage, I *thought* I had all the answers.

After work one evening, my wife walked through the door with "issues from the office". I was sitting on the screen porch, still in my shirt and tie, when she begins to vent about her day.

I listened intently as she described her day...

I listened as she described what "he said" and what "she did"...

To "reassure" her I was interested, I would occasionally respond, "Say what?" or "Say that again?" I sat there and listened for an hour… and a half...

Finally, I sat up, loosened my tie, and said, "Honey, it's okay, let's just forget about it and enjoy the evening".

Again, after an hour and a half of expressing an interest in her day…

My wife responded, "You NEVER want to listen to me!"

All together now…

We can either laugh (to ourselves) or go completely insane. However, I am proud to announce - through many years of trial and error, I finally developed a strategy – as discussed in *Put Down Your Duke's…Honey.*

Understand - when two people love and enjoy being together, then find themselves "fussing" or just not communicating, accept the notion that our "moments of disagreements" are "always" due to *The Third Element.*

THE THIRD ELEMENT

The "third element" could be any person, place or thing that influences "negative periods" in our relationship. The *Third Element* could be a situation at the office, extended family, a bad hair day, the bills, traffic, or even rain.

Having kids can be the ultimate third element, especially if they are not old enough to make their own peanut butter sandwiches.

The idea of accepting this "outside agitator" as the culprit places us in a favorable position to understand and neutralize most situations. Unless we enjoy arguing, concentrate on what's causing the static and eliminate it.

This does not give us the license to abuse the rights and privileges of our wife (and kids), - but to be able to identify the element as being positive or negative.

There could be elements that "rub us" the wrong way - directly, such as O*ur Wife's Best Friend,* which could be a positive element in disguise. It is again our objective to be able to distinguish the difference.

If we were to think-back to a particular argument (with our wives), and actually identified the "root" of the argument, we will most likely find that the root was something completely insignificant. The root could have been anything from the "outfit" she bought us – " On Sale", to *The Toilet Seat and Dirty Underwear.*

The argument "really" began because of something "that was said" during – what had begun, as a conversation, or while expressing a position on the subject. Furthermore, whatever *was* said - that sparked the argument, was said by someone who did not "think" – first.

However, of all of the negative elements that can directly affect our lives as husbands, (drum-roll please) the most challenging of them all is again, *The Power of the Movement.*

Our Brother's Keeper

The research for HG21C involved coming in contact with many professional women who happen to be wives and mothers. The conversations would cover the topics of kids, school and eventually their husbands.

Most of their "critical concerns" had to do with "how" we respond to their needs. Over time, I have learned to *listen* intently to their stories.

There were Lisa, Karen and Pamela sitting in the café' when I invited myself to sit in on the lunchtime huddle.

Of the three wives', Karen was the matriarch, having been married for more than ten years. Lisa and Pamela have each been married less than five years.

Lisa was usually the more vocal of the three. She constantly complained about how Charles, her husband, never wants to take her out, doesn't help enough with the kids, always out and when he is home, all they did was argue.

It seemed as if Lisa blamed Charles for all that was wrong with their marriage.

Waiting for my opportunity to "interject", Lisa stated, "I wish Charles was more helpful around the house, he's so lazy and never thinks about my needs". At this point, Karen's subtle glance was my queue.

One of the most thought provoking questions to wives' in this predicament is, *"How often do you make a "conscious effort" to make Charles feel good about himself"?* - Lisa froze.

While I had never met Charles, I felt their *Dilemma* was more her "doing or not doing" than his. Understand - my overall objective was to assist Charles without directly pointing the finger at Lisa. Besides, I knew the question to Lisa had given her something to think about.

This "conscious effort" question usually catches them off guard, and should eliminate the possibility of them responding with the standard "What about me"?

The Bottom line:

We should always take precautions to avoid being challenged by the "What about me?" defense. It is counter-productive and has absolutely no place in addressing our [husbands] selfish goals. Besides, if we *Understand What's Between These Lines*, she will seldom ever have any reason to feel that her "needs" are not being addressed.

A DISTANT THIRD PLACE

When we think about the responsibilities of our wives (and mother of our kids), we must accept the order of her priorities.

Realistically, the moment our wife becomes a mother, she becomes 99% mother. Which leaves us with only one-percent wife. REPEAT

We must also realize that her professional responsibilities have a great deal to do with her basic makeup as an individual. Nurturing the home is another *Element* we must consider in the equation.

With a little simple math, we must accept that her husband *could* easily be a distant third place on her list of priorities. So, we *could* appear a bit immature or even selfish when it comes to mentioning our own "needs".

Pardon me – I meant to type "wants".

<u>The Rebellious Husband</u>

Call me "selfish" if you like, - I wasn't going to stand for Third. Furthermore, if I had to wait (at least) eighteen years for only "second place" on

her list of priorities, I wasn't sure I would be patient enough to just sit on the sideline. Additionally, - I would have to be creative in my efforts to eliminate the opposition.

Take No Prisoners

Again, the kids can be the ultimate *Third Element*. Therefore, our first objective is to analyze how the kids "presently" fit into the picture, and how they can benefit our selfish goals.

I knew the most direct way to advance my position would be to get rid of the boy. However, telling our five-year-old to "get out" is against the law in "most" states.

As I looked down at my son, I knew that in order to succeed in my selfish goals, his support and cooperation would be required.

Whether we are the father of one child or five, our first objective is to recruit them onto our team. They do not "need to know" our overall "mission objective". All they need to know is – "they will be pulling a little extra-duty around the house".

However, just to be safe, we probably need to figure-in about a 50% causality rate.

54 / HG21C

The fifty-percent effort on the part of our kids has more to do with their willingness to assist. So our approach will have to be gradual.

Who are you? And, where's my Dad?

Imagine the look on our kids faces if - all of a sudden they notice us taking an active part in managing the routine chores around the house.

Our children's first instinct may be to run crying to mom saying, "Daddy is acting strange". We may even notice the kids "whispering" to each other as they attempt to understand what has come over us.

After all, from what they have observed over the years, as far as our involvement in household chores is concerned, - they would have good reason to question our sudden change as being "completely out of character".

So again, our approach must be gra-du-al. We should also be careful not to get loud and fuss, or even attempt to pull rank on the kids - if they initially resist. Fussing is counterproductive and will only prove their opinion that we have lost our minds.

56 / HG21C

$ $ $

Bribing the kids is usually the most direct way to solicit their support. And if bribing becomes a defining factor in neutralizing a particular negative element, we need to be sure to get our money's worth, - even if we are not *The Globetrotting Husband*.

The second objective is to keep an eye out for the adversaries who have the potential to become our allies. They are usually easy to recruit once they realize our intentions are honorable. *Our Wife's Best Friend* and others could over time, be our most trusted allies.

This approach "on the surface", may appear to be a bit overboard, but as we review *Commanding Respect,* we can realize - this is only a temporary strategy.

This is WAR

To define our mission is to "Get our Girl back, Giggles and all". Our prize will not be awarded overnight. "Operation GGG" will require thought, planning and patience - as in my case.

My objective was to somehow minimize my wife's responsibilities by re-assigning household duties.

I can recall the time when she complained (again) about spending all day Saturday doing the laundry, putting away clothes, etc.

My son, Tony and I had finished the yard and were heading off to Dairy Queen.

As she continued to complain, I looked her in the eyes, kissed her lips and said, "Honey, if doing the laundry is too much for you, – then you should stop doing the laundry – you're fired".

(Please, stop laughing - this is serious business.)

While some may question my decision to ban my wife from the laundry room and "not allow" her to ever do the laundry again", I needed to prove that doing the laundry was no big deal – really (?). After all, I would never complain about having to cut the grass. Again, this is WAR – and War is HELL.

Special Forces

With my son at my side, it was time for us to take action.

The duty of laundry was re-assigned to Special Forces. Tony had my back, and by the age of nine, he could separate colors, wash, dry and fold. We would routinely do the laundry during the week while watching television; Monday was white clothes while Wednesday was colors.

Of course there were "some" casualties. For about six months, all of our white clothes had a tint of red or blue – but we survived.

The Power of L.D.

I would have never imagined - the person responsible for the laundry had a position of "wisdom and power" in the house.

Think about it…how do we feel when we have to ask, "Honey, where's my blue sweatshirt"? And she answers, "Did you look in your bottom drawer" (?) - while thinking, "What an idiot".

The Lil' General

Tony also benefited from being "second in command".

There were times when Tony would announce, with great authority, "If anyone has any "darks" that need to be washed, they had better be in the laundry room by sixteen-hundred hours".

There were other times when my wife would have to "ask us" where a specific article of clothing [of hers] was...

Tony would reply, "Did you look in your bottom drawer"? While thinking…

As time went by, we also adopted the practice of using paper plates and cups to minimize washing dishes. After a short while, Tony and I developed a system whereas we would "compete or time ourselves" on picking up around the house, loading the dishwasher and other chores.

Recruiting the kids as our allies does not only assist us in our selfish goals, but it also provides the kids with the complete understanding and importance of how teamwork "works" - more so than Little League baseball.

Covert Activities
==================

Occasionally, there were some "covert missions" as well. Understand, - our objective in *some* cases was to just "appear" as if we were contributing to the household duties.

My wife and son were returning from the mall, while I was napping. As soon as the car was parked, Tony leaped from the car, pretending to rush to the bathroom. However, his objective was to alert me of their arrival and make certain I was "on duty" and not lying on my ass.

I recall on one occasion - as soon as I jumped up from my slumber, Tony tossed me the broom - just to make "us" look good.

I will admit, Tony and I *may* have gone a bit overboard, but it gave my wife the impression that she had two of the best men on earth.

62 / HG21C

CHAPTER 2

THE BUDGET OFFICER

Probably the single, most important issue in a marriage is deciding which of us will be responsible for managing the family finances and budgeting.

Let us begin by admitting - one of the many reasons we chose our spouse was not only because she was intelligent, but she also kept up with her own finances and good credit rating before we were married. Or not.

Having an intelligent wife requires a great deal of responsibility on our part. Moreover, when a person (of either gender) has a certain degree of intelligence and especially organizational skills, it should continuously be nourished so that a person will grow as an individual. To deny anyone of this opportunity would be completely un-American – to say the least.

When it comes to our wives', we need to take advantage of her "quest for intellectual growth". For example, if we were the CEO of a major corporation or even a small business, we would have a budget officer or bookkeeper to keep up with the finances. Right?

This is where we can take advantage of her need to represent the *Movement* by allowing her to exhibit her intellect. Not only is it *logical* on our part, but it will also provide her with a degree of confidence to be responsible for the most vital entity of our marital partnership. Or not.

Keeping the bills paid and maintaining a good credit rating for the both of us requires the highest level of effort and dedication. Thus the question is, "Are we better at budgeting and bookkeeping, or is she"?

<u>No Dial tone?</u>

In *my* case, I don't want the responsibility of keeping up with the bills. In fact, my only responsibility is getting the mail out of the mailbox –that's it.

My wife has done an excellent job. Our credit rating is outstanding and since she has had this responsibility, we have never had the power or telephone service disconnected, nor have we received any red flags in the mailbox.

Of course, it was different in the beginning. For some strange reason, I thought the spouse who earned the most income should have this responsibility. The problem was, "I didn't really like doing the bills". There were times when I would get behind or just forget to put the payments in the mail.

Enters: Leslie and Jackie

On a given day, Leslie would arrive home and check the mailbox. On this particular day, there was a late notice from the phone company. Leslie's reaction was – "it's okay, I mailed the bill last week".

A day or so passed and there was another late notice, this time it was from the power company. Leslie told Jackie, "It's okay, - I mailed the bill last week".

(To make a long story short…and truthful.)

I had written the checks, placed the checks and bills in their respective envelope, put the envelopes in my briefcase, - where they remained. I didn't make this discovery until the phone was disconnected.

It was then I "allowed" my wife to perform this duty and she's been managing the bills and budgeting ever since. Hey, what can I say, "She likes it".

Periodically, I will call for a "Board Meeting" in order to get "issues" out in the open or to discuss the household budget. I will admit - it is entertaining to sit down with my own personal Budget Officer and be briefed on the second quarter earnings.

Your situation may be a little different. Realistically, the person who "enjoys" maintaining the household bills is usually the better choice. Or not.

THE GLOBETROTTING HUSBAND

Let us take a moment and discuss the husband who spends most of their time away from home - living in hotels and eating meals prepared by someone named Howard - then served by another named Francis. They are the Globetrotting husbands, a special breed. On one hand, they truly enjoy their jobs. On the other hand, they live two different lives.

During my research, I was able to acquire a bit of insight into the lives of our long-distance brothers.

Admit it, you cannot wait to pack the suitcase and put it in the trunk of the car. In fact, you don't even care that you failed to pack any socks. The only hurdle now is surviving the ride to the airport.

From past events, you've learned - when "she" drives, the ride to the airport terminal is sooo… slow. Furthermore, she "chats" all the way to the passenger drop-off.

It's amazing she has the ability to turn a thirty-minute ride into an event that takes forever. So you decide - it's always best if you drive, - figuring you can save time and also minimize the time having to listen to her office war stories

Buckle-up

You peel rubber pulling out of the driveway. After all, your plane leaves in four hours – you might miss your flight.

You pull up to the terminal, put the car in park, pop the trunk, get out of the car, grab your bags and close the trunk - like a pit crew at the Indy 500.

Meanwhile, she's gets out of the car and stands there in her rollers and jogging suit waiting for the all-romantic goodbye hug and kiss.

You put your bag down and not only kiss her, but a big hug is expected. As you turn to pick up your bag, she says, "I love you, call me tonight".

Okay, so I'm over dramatizing, but you have to admit, you "do" wish the Hartsfield Gift Shop sold socks and underwear.

You're a Globetrotting husband, a special breed. And she doesn't understand that it's hard work staying in hotel after hotel, living in and out of a

suitcase - and then doing your job. In fact, no one really understands you except other globetrotters.

You pretty much live a double-life. In your business life, you perform your duties very well. For the most part, no one questions your decisions or your ability to do your job – you're great. But then you have the *other* life, that of a husband and father. And it isn't easy.

The Arrival

You're coming home after a week or so. The guy sitting next to you on the plane is also ending a week of globetrotting.

Your plane lands on time and you find yourself slowly walking through the terminal - wondering what to expect when you get home.

As you're walking through the terminal, you pass the bar and notice the guy who was sitting next to you on the plane, is now sitting at the bar - nursing his third double-scotch. He's going home too. Again, coming home isn't easy.

You find your way to the passenger pick-up and see your wife (and kids) waiting. As the kids wave, your wife pops the trunk, gets out of the car while fussing at the kids. She kisses you hello - then walks to the passenger side. She elects that you will be driving home while listening to all that you missed while you were charming Francis.

As you pull away from the airport, you say to yourself – "It's good to be home (?)".

Remember, *A Distant Third Place*?

I'm sorry to say, "Being a globetrotter doesn't make you any different than those of us on active duty".

We must also accept the fact - no matter how stressful our week was, it doesn't compare to the week of horror our wife experienced with the kids, her job and the dog. She still has her other duties and we're again, at least a distant third. So, what do we do?

Think, and remember *Sacrificing Time*.

It's the kids that are usually responsible for our rushing out the house without any socks, - not the wife. She's really on our side. So, before we retire to our "sanctuary", as discussed in *Commanding Respect*, think again. Schedule the next morning as recruitment day.

I know, it's Saturday morning, and as much as we deserve to sleep-in, we might as well shoot ourselves in the foot. Even our wife tells the kids, "Leave daddy alone and give him some peace and quiet."

While her directive to the kid's appears to have your best interest in mind, don't fall for it. And while you also believe you deserve some peace and quiet – let us take a moment to consider the following.

<u>Divide and Conquer</u>

On Saturday morning, get up early, quietly wake the kids, write the wife a note, - then grab the kids and leave. Take them to breakfast and then maybe a walk in the park. As we listen to *their* weekly highlights, we can share our own weekly highlights as well.

You'll be surprised at how this time "alone with the kids" will better our position for recruitment. Meanwhile, her morning could go something like this…

She awakens to peace and quite. At first she'll lie there wondering what day it is (?). Then she'll remember - it's Saturday, and since she doesn't hear anyone calling her name, she'll roll over and go for another thirty minutes.

When she finally gets up and finds the note on the refrigerator. She'll stand there and wonder what to do. She may stand there for fifteen minutes, confused and disoriented.

…Back to you and the kids.

As you imagine your wife standing in the kitchen and reading the note for the third time, - laugh to yourself and realize that you're a hero. In fact, for the few hours that you sacrificed (this morning), you're good for the entire weekend. But don't stop there. Remember to get your money's worth.

Before you return to the house, let the kids in on how they contributed to mom getting some "chill time" and that they are heroes (too). Give them the cell phone and have them call mom to ask if she needs anything special from the grocery store. You're in like Flint.

Meanwhile, back at the ranch.

The wife has recovered from her trance and is probably getting dressed, putting on makeup and has time to think about "tonight". Who knows, she might even "giggle".

Just think - later, we can take a nap, play 18 holes or watch the game.

GET A GIRLFRIEND

While HG21C has discussed a few negative elements of the *Movement,* let us take a look at a positive one. "Women are everywhere" - from the cafeterias, to the boardrooms, to the police force. Bless their hearts.

With this over-abundance of feminine charm and perfume all around us, we must admit that God Almighty has truly blessed us with the gift of woman. - We only had to sacrifice a rib. And with this gift, comes a great deal of responsibility and especially discipline. So…

Not a girlfriend - "girlfriend", I am referring to an ally. She could be a neighbor, co-worker or a wife of a friend. She could also assist us in choosing the appropriate birthday or Christmas gift.

Finding the *right* girlfriend is important. She must have pretty much the same style and taste as our wives. Older women will make the best advisors because they are sympathetic to the "needs" of women based on their own life experiences. In addition, they will not put the wife in the position to question our intentions.

Our "girlfriend" could also be *that* last minute babysitter in case we want to take the wife on a surprise weekend getaway or to just get rid of the kids for the evening.

Having a girlfriend as an advisor, will allow us to be more confident in sensing what approach to take in a given circumstance.

When other women believe our most important objective is to be a better husband, our advisors will be more than happy to assist us in almost any situation. Rest assured - we will never miss another birthday or anniversary again.

Our WIFE vs. Our BEST Friend

We all have our best golf buddy or long time childhood friend. They provide us with the so-called "male bonding" type of relationship that we need to keep us in the mind-set of being men. They also provide us with the level of comfort to completely be ourselves. Our best friend could also, unfortunately, be our wives' worst enemy.

One of the reasons "why" she feels this way is because our "best friend" has the ability to bring out a personality in us that our wife doesn't know, or even hates.

It's easy to understand if we accept the notion - that as human beings, *some* people have the ability to alter our personalities, good or bad.

James and Mike had been friends since high school. They were also college roommates and are now in their mid-thirties. In fact, Mike was James's best man.

James has been married to Pamela for three years while Mike is still single and has always had a reputation of being a ladies man.

When James and Pamela were dating, they would occasionally double date with Mike and his seasonal favorite. Pamela however, never took Mike's girlfriends seriously because it was a different woman every month.

Pamela had accepted Mike and James's longtime friendship, but often felt uncomfortable when the two of them were out playing golf or just out. Her concerns were understandable, knowing Mike's reputation with the ladies.

James sensed Pamela's discomfort but never really considered her feelings as legitimate. Even when he would get home late from "happy hour", Pamela said very little.

The problems started when Mike asked James and Pamela to "cover" for him by lying to his present girlfriend, saying - he was at their house playing cards the night before. Pamela refused.

While James was supportive of Mike's request to "cover", Pamela insisted - she would not have any part of it. James didn't think it was a big deal and questioned Pamela's decision not to go along. After all, it was Mikey.

We could take this story further, but it's no need. What James didn't realize was that his participation in covering for Mike was a big mistake.

James should have never, I repeat, never (!) have asked his wife to cover for his buddy. Additionally, James did not realize, that covering for Mike, jeopardized his integrity in the eyes of his wife, Pamela.

James just wasn't "thinking".

The moral of this story is, - if we have a friend or acquaintance that influences us to have the type of behavior that our wife does not approve, we need to do whatever it takes to neutralize it.

This can be done in one of two ways.

Our first and most logical approach should be to express to our friend that "our wife comes first". Let him know "what he does" that irritates our wife most, and ask him to adjust his behavior by accommodating our wishes. If he is truly our friend, and has our best interest in mind, he will modify his behavior.

The other, unfortunate approach is to acknowledge that his friendship is not worth the bother and "minimize" the relationship. Believe me, he's not worth jeopardizing the harmony of our Empires or especially, the relationship with our wives.

CHAPTER 3

He's SO SENSITIVE

I have no idea why women today seem to assert an appreciation for a "sensitive man". The term itself is basically an insult to our manhood. However, if we were to make an effort to "try" and understand what their intentions are, I would say, that it's basically a trend. A trend, that is intended to "de-masculinize" (if you will) men, for the sake of the *Movement*.

As unreasonable as this may sound, my only suggestion is again to *Understand What's Between These Lines*.

Over the years, I have approached women on this subject and have found varying definitions. The definition I believe is the most appropriate for us to consider falls into the category of [us] making an effort to "express an interest" in the issues that are important to our wives.

When it comes to our wives', "an important issue" could be as simple as furnishing the bedroom or den. The interest could also be as serious as her job, or an ingrown hair. So the question is, "Does our wife feel - we sincerely have an interest in what's important to her?" The fact is – we should.

Expressing an interest in our wife's personal issues is in no way traditional, and is not a "direct responsibility" [of ours]. But, if we fail to do so, it *will* create consequences – like a two-by-four, right between the eyes.

For example, if we were to recall *Making a Conscious Effort* - it describes a wife and her male co-worker and how "he" expresses an interest in her personal "needs". Another example of an "indirect consequences" could be to experience living with a woman that, in our opinion, is…

The Telephone Queen

Talking "too much" on the telephone is a vice most women go through from time to time. The fact is, they like to talk. But most of all, they like to be "listened to" more. REPEAT

However, if your wife spends more time on the phone than you "wish", - there *is* a problem. This doesn't mean we have the "right to demand" that she minimizes her time talking to her friends, but rather, she should be more considerate to our wishes.

If this is a problem in your Empire, you have probably made some sort of effort to eliminate it, but unsuccessfully.

Our approach must be thoughtful and considerate. In other words, we can't say, - "You spend too much time on the phone - Honey", without having a strategy.

<u>Filling the Void</u>

It has been my experience - if there *is* a problem, our first step is to "think" about a way to fill the void - which the telephone is now filling. Filling the void *may* be as simple (?) as "teaching ourselves" to listen to her more. But I must warn you, be prepared for a challenge that may be more than we can handle overnight.

[Think]

If our wife is spending time talking to a relative such as her mother or sister, we should leave things the way they are. However, if she spends hours talking to someone "we believe" - has a negative influence on her ability to be a loving wife and mother, we must take action!

HG21C Sidebar:

As we review *He's SO Sensitive,* it is important - we position ourselves to avoid the "slightest possibility" of her being able to utilize the "What about me?" defense. Right? - Right.

Checking Ourselves

Checking ourselves "first" must be considered in our assault on the "institution of female bonding", - Because the reason she spends all that time on the phone *may* be because we have not convinced her - we sincerely care about the issues that are important to her.

I have found that making a conscious effort to schedule "talk time" with the wife is an approach, which can eventually minimize her time on the telephone. We [you] could start with as little as 15 to 20 minutes a day. As time goes on, you could be surprised that we actually enjoy the conversations (?).

HOUSEHOLD CHORES and the SUPER BOWL

Sit back and think of the days when we were single. Yeah…back to the days when we had our first apartment. We had the ultimate bachelor pad, - milk crate bookcases and cheap art. Also remember "who" was responsible for keeping the "pad" clean?

We washed our own clothes, cleaned the bathroom, washed the dishes, made up the bed and kept the magazines stacked neatly on the coffee table. After all, back in those days, we were motivated.

It's Friday night, and we're expecting "company for the evening". She rings the bell, - the evening was under way. Our only concern is hoping we did not forget to lower the toilet seat.

All right, let's get back to "today" and discuss the issue of household chores "logically".

Unless our wife was "raised by wolves", she has pretty much accepted the responsibility of preparing the meals and taking care of most of the household chores. After all, it's in her nature to do so.

The problem is - if we are "allowing" her to be responsible for most of the household duties, we are being set up – big time. *This is War,* - we might as well "shoot ourselves in the foot – again". And if we have kids, their opinion of us is less than respectable because our wife is letting it be known to all, that she's doing everything "by herself" and we are no help.

The fact is, many of us "help out" all the time. The problem is, she really "feels" that she is doing more. And until we "out-perform" her, she will continue to "feel" this way. REPEAT

The Bottom Line:

Whether it's watching "the game", playing 18 holes, or taking a mid-afternoon nap, we should be able to enjoy these activities without *anyone* "questioning" whether or not we are deserving.

I believe again, that *Sacrificing Time* is in order, or we can think about this topic the next time we're sitting on our asses watching the game. *Sorry.*

HG21C / 89

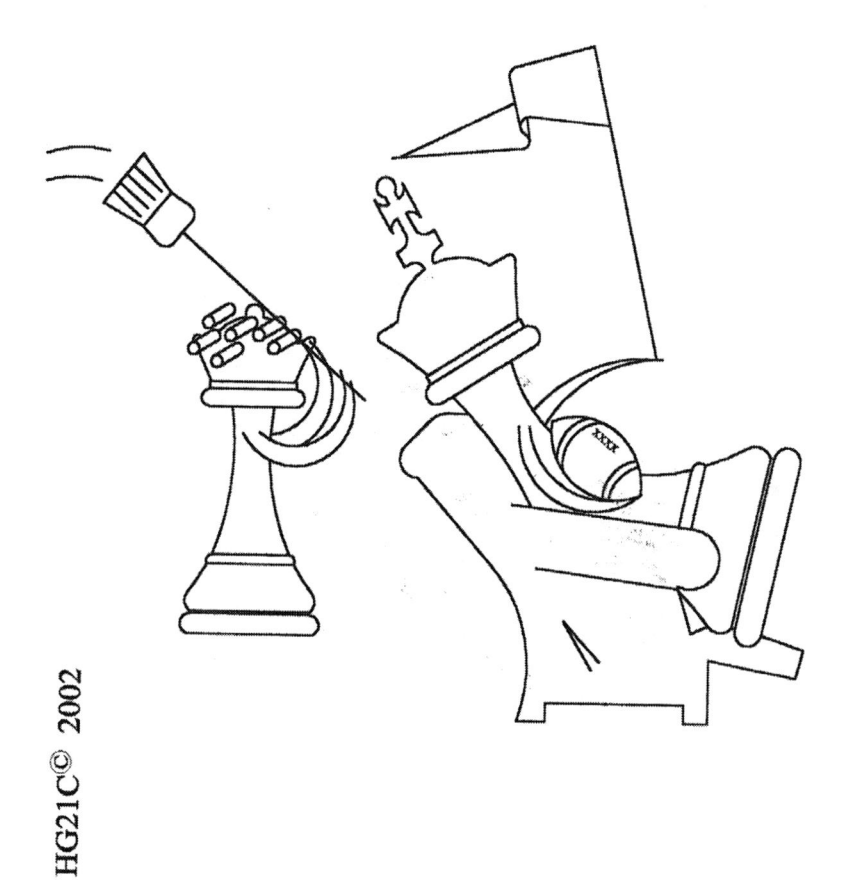

HG21C© 2002

I'm NOT ROMANTIC Anymore (?)

I'm sure you agree, - this is a "tough one". I will admit that this topic would have been "tougher" to neutralize, had it not been for our friend (?) - the *Dictionary*.

Romance (rō-māns') **1.** A love affair, **2.** To make romantic love, **3.** A strong, usually short-lived attachment or enthusiasm.

Pick one. I dare you.

It seems as if our wives' have (re) defined this term for one of four (or more) reasons.

1) To make us feel as if "we don't love and/or appreciate them" – like we use to; or
2) They want us to buy them "stuff" – flowers, diamonds;
3) Take them out dancing "more";
4) Etc …etc… etc.

During my research, "the above" was pretty much how our wives defended their accusations that, "We're not romantic anymore".

Many of us are faced with this "accusation" after about three years of marriage, or within a year (or so) after our first child was born.

Just between us guy's...

I could never really master the art of romance, especially after twenty years of marriage. Truthfully, I have always felt that definition number "3" is the "truest definition" of romance – "short lived".

This is not to say that I no longer love and appreciate my wife, I truly "do". My problem is - I have always been "too [damn] logical" to accept the term as *they* wish to define it.

When it comes to expressing *my* love and affection towards my wife, I have chosen to be "charming".

Charmer (chärmer) **1.** One who is alluring or pleasing. **2.** To attract or delight greatly. **3.** Having the power to charm, especially a woman.

Again, just between us guy's.

To be charming, is truly an art, which requires skill and many years of practice. Once we have acquired the power to charm, we must learn to "use it for good and not evil". It's not only powerful, but it's also cheaper.

Besides the "cheaper remark", our wife would appreciate being "charmed" - more so than being romanced. Thus, the term *Romance* can easily be neutralized by acknowledging - it is basically "fantasy", that only survives in the movies and romance novels. So again, our efforts should be focused more on "charming (the pants off of) her".

Believe me, we should take advantage of every opportunity.

Tell her how nice she looks – before she leaves for work in the morning. (3 seconds)

Leaving her little "notes". (30 seconds)

Call her at the office at least once a week, just to tell her, – "I just wanted to hear your voice" or "I love you". (3 minutes)

Sending her flowers for no reason. ($$)

Never end a day without - a hug, (5 seconds), or rubbing her fanny. (59 seconds)

The Bottom Line:

While there are many different kinds of women, with varying "needs", they all have the sincere desire to be (re) assured that we love and appreciate them – the way we use to.

Why not? – It only takes a few moments a day and an occasional seventy-five bucks.

The TOILET SEAT & DIRTY UNDERWEAR

At a very early age we were taught to raise the toilet seat. In fact, learning to raise the toilet seat was one of our first major lessons in [life] becoming responsible men. The only problem with this directive was - our parents failed to express to us, the importance of lowering the seat.

As we grew older, this all-important task of raising the toilet seat became second nature and completely instinctive. Moreover, we thought the issue of the toilet seat was behind us, - until we got married.

Now we are faced with the greatest challenge of all, - learning to lower the seat for the convenience of our wives'.

Thinking…

Now… it would seem that when our wives were little girls, they would have learned to "check the seat" – first. However it's apparent that her parents failed to teach her the importance of checking the toilet seat –before she sat down. And somehow, we are now blamed when our wives' experience the feeling of cold porcelain on their [lovely] behinds.

We must admit, imagining the look of "anyone" stuck in the toilet, is quite humorous – to say the least.

Another "serious issue" that has been brought to our attention is how we leave our socks and dirty underwear on the floor. From our point of view, it's no big deal. However, to our wives', it appears to them that our parents - failed in this respect.

In fact, our wives have no problem with telling the world - we [husbands] are slobs and also question how our mother's could have allowed this "unspeakable behavior".

On the other hand, we say nothing when our wives', after a day at the office, kicks off her high-heeled shoes in the middle of the kitchen floor, or the mess (comb, brush, lipstick, curling iron, mascara, etc.) she leaves on the bathroom vanity. To us again, it's no big deal.

In the whole scheme of things, we could honestly take credit for being "more understanding" by accepting our spouses as occasionally being "equal".

Back to the Toilet Seat

When it comes to "who is responsible" for the position of the toilet seat, logic tells us that everyone should lower the toilet seats before leaving the bathroom - period.

If it makes you feel any better. The next time she complains about dirty underwear on the floor, - just apologize and imagine how she looks with her ass stuck in the toilet. Bless her heart.

The Bottom Line:

For the sake of fairness and "equal status" in the household, it's apparent - we have to recognize that over time, husbands and wives have evolved into equal slobs. And after we consider the information mentioned in *This is War,* we would feel better to realize - we're not the only one's with dirty underwear.

PUT DOWN YOUR DUKES…HONEY

No matter what kind of job or profession our wife has, chances are good that "she brings it home". She just can't seem to shake it off during her drive home. She walks in the house with her "dukes up" and until she "vents", we'll just have to stand there and pretend as if we care.

Before we delve deeper into this topic…

We must admit that traditionally, [men] have been conditioned to leave our issues at the office. Thus, when we do "vent", it is usually inspired by the "How was your day" or "What's wrong with you" question.

As mentioned in *"Damned if I do, Damned if I Don't",* I learned quite a bit during that era. Please allow me to share a "modified approach".

During that period, I "thought" sharing my day was a healthy approach - NOT. The fact is, if our issues are not as controversial as her issues from the office, "*she*" could give a damn" - understandably.

As confusing as it may seem, we cannot afford to make this issue more complicated than it really is.

HG21C / 99

The fact is, we must always be there for our wives. And in this case, all we have to do is sacrifice a little time - by listening.

Listening has many advantages, such as when we attend our wife's company picnic. In that, we will be able to put a "face to the names" of the troublemakers responsible for delaying our reading room appointment. This insight will also contribute greatly to *Christmas Parties and the Ride Home*.

Seeking the Motivation

When it comes to seeking the motivation to listen intently to our wife's war stories, most of us will be surprised of what we can learn from our wife's experiences at the office, – from a "woman's point of view". REPEAT

That's right, we can learn a great deal about *our* female co-workers by listening to our wives.

Of course the motivation can only take us so far.

Severe Abdominal Pains

When we find ourselves becoming "disinterested", it is important we take action immediately, - before our facial expression gives us away. When this occurs, our first step should be to:

1) Avoid eye contact. Our eyes will give us away every time, especially when our eyes begin to tear.

2) Next, gently reach out, slowly turn her around and rub her back and shoulders – like the prizefighter she is. Then,

3) Give her a hug and say, "They don't appreciate you – like I do", and/or, "I'm so proud of you honey".

4) Pause for a moment…then kiss the back of her neck. Then freeze…

If we're lucky, she will "back-off", remove her boxing gloves and we can finally grab the newspaper and make our appointment. The workday is over. Or…

THE STEPFATHER

Being a stepfather has special *elements* that can increase the odds of us "not" being a successful husband (and father). No matter what the ages of *her* children, they will eventually rebel [against us] by utilizing those famous words "You're not my real father". Moreover, having to "share their mom", with anyone - could be considered the ultimate sacrifice to a ten-year-old.

Their rebellion however, should not be taken personal. Children, and especially teenagers are blessed with the natural instinct "to rebel". And in our case, they have the leverage to take advantage of our status. Or course – to neutralize this challenge, all we have to do is refer to *Commanding Respect.*

The *real* problems occur when we do not have the support and respect of our wife - their mother. Even if our wife disagrees with our methods as a father, she has the responsibility to - at least, appear to the children, to stand beside us.

Let us assume that - before we chose a wife-with-children, we considered a few of the additional challenges that come with accepting the responsibility of being a stepfather.

Strike One

First of all, we married (or marrying) a "mother" - not a wife. Please forgive the directness, but this "statement of fact" must be considered.

As we review "*A Distant Third Place*", we will be able to accept the notion, "When a woman becomes a mother, she becomes 99% mother".

Strike Two

The next challenge is to anticipate some degree of interference from the biological father and/or his family. Whether their interference is positive or negative, it is an *element* that must be considered as we attempt to be a "father figure" to the child (or children).

Strike Three

The third issue that needs to be considered is how "our family" will accept our choice of a wife-with-children. For example, while our parents (step-grandparents) will accept the choice we have made, our expectations of their affections towards the step-grandchildren could be more than they can deliver.

In other words, if our parents have other (blood-related) grandchildren, we will "expect" them to express (to their step-grandchildren) the same love and affection. Again, our expectations could be quite high, and in some cases completely unreasonable. So, if we are considering a wife-with-children, make certain we look at the big picture and know what to expect.

On the other hand, if we are presently a stepfather, we have already realized - these "top three" challenges require a considerable amount of understanding on our part and more importantly complete support from our wife.

Grand slam

Support from our wife is the key to being or becoming a successful stepfather and husband. Moreover, "how" she supports and (especially) respects us as the "man of the house," will be the foundation to our success.

Acquiring the support and respect of our wife (and children) is again, an effort in *Commanding Respect* - rather than "demanding" respect. After all, there is a distinct difference.

CHAPTER 4

COMMANDING RESPECT

In everything we do as men, having our integrity in tact is - by far, our most important responsibility. We owe it not only to our families, but to our communities as well.

Furthermore, to embark into this century without considering the social changes as they occur, - we are destined to fail. - Especially when it comes to being a husband and the head of the household.

We are probably the first generation of husbands who can no longer establish our rules or ideals, with regard to managing the home. Our fathers, grandfathers and Archie Bunker had the complete support of their wives and society as a whole.

Our generation however, is experiencing an ever-changing society that we must consider when we take the position of managing our Empires.

The "basic approach" to effectively be the head of the household will require a great deal of "savvy management" and most importantly, "how we present ourselves" to our family. After all, our family's opinion of us should (logically) be the most important issue in our lives. With this said, we must first acquire the motivation.

Searching for our own motivation to "re-invent" our priorities, with regard to managing our homes can vary depending on our specific situation. *My motivation is based on a statement made by my late grandfather when I was around ten years old.*

I paraphrase:

"When in public, always conduct yourself as if you are being observed, because in most cases you are (being observed)".
- William F. Bell, Sr.

I did not truly understand the significance of these words – with regard to being a husband (and father), until I had been married for more than ten years. I found the "key words" in that statement are *"When in public"*. Thus, when we are in the company of anyone, including our family, we are [in fact] in public.

HG21C Sidebar:

If we were to examine the subject of defining our true personalities, I would say, "we are truly ourselves", only when we are "alone". This will conflict with the idea that being at home should be "the place" where we can relax and reveal our true selves.

The idea of "when" we are truly our selves is worthy of consideration. And unless we have our own personal sanctuary at home, such as a den, basement or garage, we could be considered a man without peace and solitude.

Sanctuary Therapy

Men have traditionally had a place of sanctuary - at home. We can usually retreat to this area when we have a legitimate hobby or particular interest. Some [men] can find this solitude by not entering the home until we have inspected the lawn, practice putting in the yard or to sit in the car/garage pretending to listen to the news.

It is important that our "place of sanctuary" be just that – "our place". Like a damp and musty "unfinished" basement, for example. She may insist that we can afford to finish the basement with carpeting, framed art, and new furniture. Don't fall for it. Or the next thing we know – scented candles.

The only drawback in utilizing *"sanctuary therapy"* is - we can easily abuse it by never coming out [in public].

Commanding respect from our wife, has a great deal to do with minimizing any negative opinions she may have of us. HG21C is not suggesting we can change our habits overnight. After all, it has taken years of practice for us to master the art of being ourselves.

What HG21C is suggesting, - take note of the things "we do" (or don't do) that she may find questionable or perhaps goofy. These "things" could be anything from - leaving dirty clothes or dishes lying around, to not putting on a shirt when we have company (?).

Over time, we will find that most of our modifications will be very simple tasks, as discussed in *Sacrificing Time*.

However – in the event we notice "she also" has some habits that "we" find questionable, by all means, say nothing. - I repeat, "Say nothing". But rather, save it for the sake of having a defense when we do something "really stupid". Believe me, we'll need it.

The Bottom line:

We will find that being dedicated and consistent in managing the home could neutralize anyone questioning our decisions. But again, we must be fair and objective in our decisions and most importantly, knowing when to "allow" or delegate a particular decision to another family member.

Whatever our "motivation", it will require the complete understanding that our wife and children are looking to us to be a fair and responsible manager of the home.

112 / HG21C

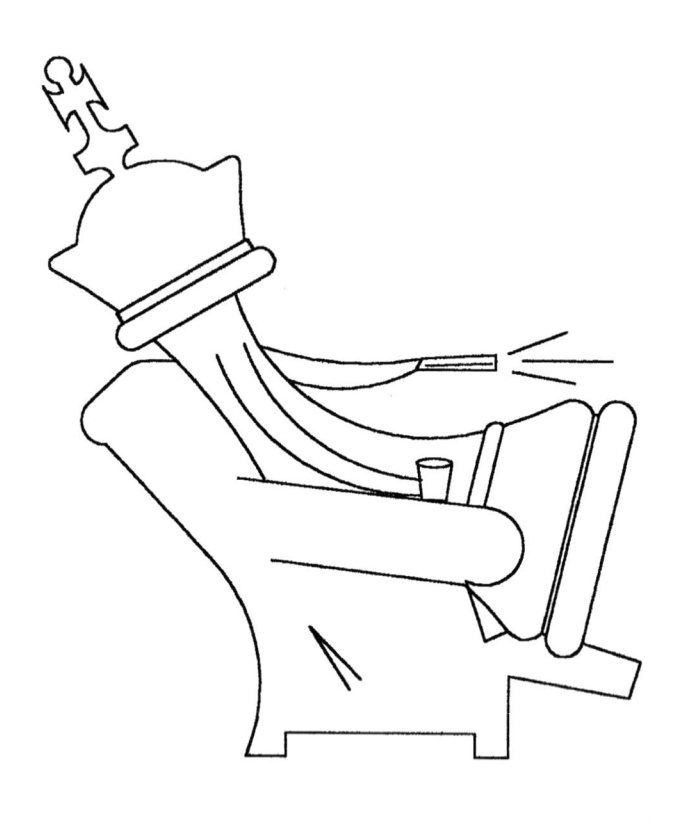

WHEN DECISIONS BECOME REGRETS

The next time we're sitting in our recliner, remote in one hand and a glass of sherry (or Beer) in the other, look around - take it all in.

It's Sunday evening, we just finished a great meal, and the kids are upstairs preparing for another week of school. As we're taking it all in, realize that in order to continue to enjoy the simple, settled life, we must continuously work on it.

What's most important, we must realize - we could lose it all by making a decision that becomes a life-long regret.

<u>Alternative Relationships</u>

As we consider the temptations many of us face from time to time with regard to other women and their feminine charms - we must always be on guard. This is one element that can ruin more than just our families – directly, but can also have a devastating affect on our children's children.

The following story is a prime example.

Greg had been married to Karen for nearly ten years. They also had two sons, ages seven and five.

Karen had been a housewife until their 5 year old began kindergarten.

Karen and Greg were both active in little league sports activities like most parents, and were also members of the Community Church where their oldest son was a Scout.

Karen was excited about her new job, while Greg found himself becoming a distant third place on Karen's list of priorities. It was not long before Greg found himself vulnerable to the charms of another women.

Greg had always been a dedicated husband and father until he found himself becoming attracted to Barbara, a co-worker also married. The two of them often spent lunch hours together as well as staying late at the office. Then it happened. - BOOM.

When the dust settled, Karen was awarded the house, the car, and the kids. Meanwhile, Greg was ordered by the court to pay more than half of his salary in alimony and child support.

While Karen was the best mother she could be, she could not control the boys when they became teenagers. By the time their oldest son was fifteen, he had dropped out of school, was in and out of trouble, and had also become a father at the age of seventeen.

By the time the younger son reached sixteen, he was also involved in various crimes such as destruction of private property, vandalism and car theft. - All they needed was their dad.

It is unfortunate HG21C was not available to Greg when his wife and sons were depending on him to be resistant to the temptations that most of us could face.

To acknowledge the "power of feminine charms", we can all take precautions to avoid putting ourselves in a position of becoming guilty of disrupting the futures of so many innocent victims – like the kids.

Not to mention – the uncertain future of Greg and Karen's grandchild.

While many of us can understand Greg and his need for feminine charms, we must all learn from his decision - that was, not only a lifelong regret, but also destroyed the future generations of his family.

On the other hand, we can applaud those of us that have overcome the temptations.

<u>Guys like Mike.</u>

Mike and Tricia had been married for three years and soon became the parents of a lovely daughter.

One summer afternoon, while Mike was lunching with Mary, his co-worker, he noticed that he had acquired an attraction for Mary, and she of him. They would often flirt with each other at the office, but neither realized they were approaching the threshold of temptation.

Mary was also married. Her husband was a globetrotter and out of town for weeks at time. She would occasionally travel with her husband, but never enjoyed hotel living.

It was Mary that made the first move. She had expressed to Mike - she often fantasized about them being together. Mike also confessed to Mary about his thoughts of them becoming intimate.

While Mike had expressed an interest in Mary, he had no intention of violating his vows and wanted to be sure Mary understood. Mary on the other

hand was making plans to fulfill her fantasies.
PAUSE

HG21C Sidebar:

Generally, for a *husband* to have a friend – who happens to be female, is no way traditional. We usually begin these relationships via our working environments and can occasionally, carry over to our social or even our family lives.

During my research, many wives admitted they have no problem with their husbands having female friends. However, when their husbands become obsessed with mentioning "her" name more so than his buddy Pete, they [wives] become concerned - understandably.

While my research did not include this topic to husbands, I am certain we would feel the same way if our wives began to repeatedly mention the "new man in her life".

Dancing with Landmines

Having an attraction to females - other than our wives is fairly understandable, especially when we again mention, "women are everywhere".

Therefore, it is our responsibility to draw the line in the sand and just dance on one side (?).

However, even to dance without crossing the line, could still be a violation – if our wife were to find out that another woman has the ability to "make us feel good about our selves".

It would seem that our working environments have somehow become "hazardous" with more than a few "landmines". Our only advantage is the landmines are visible, wears perfume and high-heel shoes.

HG21C Sidebar:

During my research, most wives, made it clear - I should "never call them at home", but rather their office. As I recall this period, it is interesting and clear "they too" were in violation – because [husbands] we *would* not have approved.

This information is not only interesting, but also tells us that women, and perhaps our wives, have mastered the art of keeping a small portion of their lives private. After all, unless we married idiots, our wives are basically smarter than we will ever be.

To acknowledge the level of intelligence of our wives is a notion many of us must accept. We must also accept the fact - from the moment they awaken, they immediately begin to think (and speak). We [men] however, need a shower, two cups of coffee and twenty minutes in rush hour traffic before we realize the day of the week.

As we summarize the subject of "dancing" without crossing the line, we must remember - unless we lock ourselves in the men's room stall, we are always being observed.

Back to Mike and the Landmine

It was important to Mike that he communicate his "honorable intentions" to Mary without ruining their friendship or disrupting their ability to work together. Mike also understood - he must set the record straight, before Mary made her move.

However, Mary made her move first by mentioning to Mike - she would like to see him after work during the periods when her husband was out of town.

Mike responded.

"Mary, we must be extremely careful. There are many innocent people that would be hurt if we choose to make decisions that we will one day regret". Mike added, "I have a great deal of respect and affection for you and would hate to ruin our relationship by becoming intimate".

Although Mary was disappointed, she knew he loved his wife and daughter and that Mike also had the integrity to set the record straight.

Over time, Mary became a family friend. She, Tricia and the baby became shopping buddies. Mike was happy, and so were his girls.

The Bottom Line:

Being involved in an alternate relationship is indeed, an "element" we should all avoid. Again, it is usually the downfall of not only our marriages, but also the future of our kids, and grandkids.

There are many available women out there whose "mission in life" is to break up marriages, just for the sport of it. So, before we even consider an alternative relationship, "think" and remember, "regrets" are mistakes that can't be corrected.

Spousal Abuse

It would have been too easy to research and gather statistics on this topic. So I didn't.

In fact, I would prefer - not to even discuss the physical abuse of women at all. And I am certain, the readers of HG21C are not the "wife-beater" types - anyway.

With this said, I will just keep it short, - "Don't do it".

However, one does not have to get physical to be abusive.

Samuel and Gloria had been married for around ten years and were the parents of one son – six, a daughter ten and were expecting their third.

The bills were piling up and Samuel often blamed Gloria for not earning any income, because she chose to stay at home with the kids – as she and Samuel agreed.

One day Samuel began to express his opinion that Gloria was not "doing enough" and said, "I don't know why I ever married you". Etc...(30 seconds)

Gloria had endured many of Samuel's tantrums, but this time was truly the worst.

As time passed, Samuel had "forgotten" what he had said that day, and the loving spirit that Gloria lost, was replaced with periods of crying and depression. - Gloria never forgot.

Again, I would prefer not to discuss or even attempt to understand how one could abuse their wives and the mother of their children.

<u>Walking on Eggshells</u>

What's more disturbing is – of all the topics discussed in HG21C, it was impossible for me to (cleverly) find any "comedy in this tragedy".

As I sit here pondering "what to write next", - I am guessing at least one of us *have* "smacked her in the mouth" for what seemed to be – "the right thing to do at the time". Thus, I am walking on eggshells.

Derrick's Dilemma

When Derrick was a boy growing up in Indiana, his dad physically abused his mom for many years. This experience has cause Derrick to have an "extremely" negative opinion of men that beat-up woman.

I truly believe - if there were a Company or Profession that involved "beating up wife-beater's", Derrick would take the job, even if the job paid "minimum wage".

Moreover, with Derrick having earned his MBA, I am certain he would have the "business savvy" to capitalized on this growth-industry.

Imagine, next to every fast food restaurant:" Husband Beaters Incorporated". - With the slogan, "Don't call the Cops, Call H.B.I.".

Derrick and Susan have been married for ten years and are both professionals in their mid-forties. Every month or so, they get together with other couples and "hang out".

After a couple of hours, and three gin and tonics, Susan would get LOUD and begin to challenge

Derrick's every word. She would get louder and LOUDER as the evening progressed.

As all witnessed – Susan pointing her finger in Derrick's face, it seemed as if she was "testing" the limits of Derrick's tolerance by mentioning many of his personal habits that should be considered private.

Pardon me…I forgot to mention, - Derrick is six feet and weighs around 210. Susan is less than five feet and weighs about as much as the average ten-year-old.

As fellow husbands, we can only support Derrick by taking up a collection and hiring two five-year-old little girls to give Susan the "ass kicking" she deserves. Of course the *Logical* approach would be to hide the gin.

Crack…Crack

As the eggshells began to crack beneath my feet, I must defend my position by stating that "some wives", believe they *are* victims, - as they attempt to put lipstick on a fat lip or mascara on a black eye. – Perhaps most are victims (?).

However, in Derrick's case, - Those who know him would support him should he ever be arrested for offering money to solicit the services of two K5 hit-girls.

- Good luck Derrick.

THE STAY-AT-HOME DAD

We must all question this title for the mere reason - no real man can stay home and/or just watch the kids. Excuse my prejudice, but this term can be confusing to the logical mind.

In support of my opinion, or for the sake of argument, - Have you ever heard of a "Stay at home Husband"?

A man:

May have the convenience of "working" from home,

May drop-off and pick-up the kids, and

May perform most of the household chores.

But a "Stay at Home Dad"? - Give me a break. Let's give this guy the title that he deserves:

Super Husband

We can only advise the Super Husband to be patient and take plenty of vitamins. Like everything else in life, it's temporary.

This is especially true when it comes to the relationship with the kids.

Paul and Carol had been married for nearly fourteen years and were the parents of an eleven-year-old son, Jason.

Carol was a nurse working 12-hour shifts, which meant that Paul was responsible for getting Jason up in the mornings, preparing breakfast and dropping him off at school.

Jason enjoyed riding to and from school with his dad. After school, they would often pick up Chinese food for dinner while watching television together. Paul also enjoyed spending time with Jason. They had become pretty good friends.

However, when Jason started high school, the enjoyment of being dropped off and picked up by his dad had become embarrassing.

Tim, one of Jason's classmates lived in the neighborhood and rode to school with his older sister, a senior.

At the age of fifteen, Jason wanted to ride with the teenagers and asked his dad for permission. Paul had to except - Jason was growing up and was making his first attempt to become independent. So Paul agreed, but after a week of Jason riding with friends, the father began to miss his son. PAUSE

The Adventures of Super Husband

Paul had one great advantage, he knew his son, - they were more than just father and son, they were buddies. Paul knew that over the past few years while getting Jason ready for school, preparing meals and just "hanging out", he was prepared to take advantage of "knowing his son". So Paul decided - it was time for driving lessons.

The next Saturday morning, Paul took Jason to an empty parking lot and handed him the steering wheel. Paul could tell by the excitement on Jason's face that he had his son back. From that time on, Jason preferred to ride with dad while learning to drive.

While this story may be more related to being a father, it also provides us with a little insight of the advantages of being a "stay-at-home-dad" – Pardon me, a *Super Husband*.

Over the years, Jason had observed his dad "taking charge" of managing the home. And together they took care of Carol.

So, before we attempt to believe that being a *Super Husband* is "hard labor", we can realize that if he plays his cards right, he could be in a very lucrative position. As long as the *Super Husband* has his health, he can pretty much dictate the rules of his Empire without any resistance from the status quo.

Please allow me to rephrase.

Having a wife with a work schedule that will not allow her to participate in the daily routines of managing the home and the kids - could create some advantages to the Super Husband. In fact, he's probably happier than most of us can imagine.

Although temporary, the efforts of the S.H. "should" (theoretically) produce the kind of wife that is less stressed, which could enable her to pay more attention to being a more companionate and attentive wife. Or not.

CHRISTMAS PARTIES and the RIDE HOME

Most of us realize the importance of attending office parties and picnics. Our attendance to these events could have quite an impact on the future of our careers. Thus, we must attend.

Whether it was the annual company picnic or the Christmas party, the ride home always ends in an argument. And for those of us that have memories of the "ride home" – we have a few questions:

1) Why am I always blamed for saying, not saying, doing or not doing "something" at the party?
2) When it's my wife's company function, can I just become gravely ill, and she stays home to nurse me back to health?
3) And so on...

The fact is, no matter whose company function it is, the evening ends as a "prelude to war". Even in the old days when office functions were mostly "his" office function, the ride home ended the same way. Why?

The answer is *Logically* simple.

When we are in our "working environment", or in the company of co-workers, we all adopt a totally different personality. And "that personality" is in no way the same personality that's known to our spouses. We *could* call it Environmental Influence (E.I.) or more directly – another *Third Element*.

I have no idea whether E.I. is a "studied social science", but it fits. E.I. could also apply when the "function" is populated by only one of the spouse's friends or associates.

Paul was at his desk one afternoon when his boss stopped by to invite he and his wife Carol to dinner – in celebration of a new client. Paul immediately called his wife Carol to allow her time to adjust her schedule and contact a babysitter.

They all met at Bennihana's, a popular Japanese restaurant in midtown. This was not the first time the department had dinner together, - so many of the other spouses had met at prior gatherings, except Carol.

By the time Paul and Carol had arrived, most were finishing their first round of cocktails, while ordering their second. After a few moments of introductions, Carol ordered a Shirley Temple, while Paul ordered a double-scotch – to catch up with everyone else.

There were many inside jokes among the celebrating co-workers, while the spouses observed. However, Carol was not having a good time.

As Carol nursed the same Shirley Temple all evening, she began to see Paul as - totally out of character, than her loving husband. As the evening past, Paul would occasionally ask Carol, "Are you okay - honey?"

As the evening ended, while walking to the car, Paul again, asked Carol was she alright (?). Carol remained silent until they pulled into their garage – then she "went off".

…Carol ended her moment of rage with "I'll NEVER go to any more of your office parties again". And to this day, Paul has no idea what happened.

Paul and Carol had only been married a few years when this occurred and for the next five years, they never attended another office function together. And Paul has not received a promotion in nearly five years.

What-to-do, what-to-do?

Again, we should all attend our wife's office functions because it's the right thing to do. (Sorry)

One popular and successful approach is – where couples agree to limit their time at these events by practicing the "cameo appearance" approach. - Thirty minutes tops.

We could also take a selfish approach to finding the motivation - by "making a deal" with the wife in which "she agrees" to prepare drinks and sandwiches for you and your guests at your next Super Bowl Party. And if she resists, go to *Sacrificing Time.*

SACRIFICING TIME

For those of us that have volunteered our time as Scout Masters, coaches, or building a home for Habitat for Humanity, we cannot express the joy and satisfaction in sacrificing our time. It's priceless.

A good example would be to spend fifteen minutes every evening reviewing our kid's homework assignments - dad. Then spend another ten minutes telling the kids about the idiots at the office.

Sacrificing our time is probably the most inexpensive investment we can make in almost any situation. Especially when we compare the "time sacrificed" to the unlimited rewards.

This is basically a question of how much we are willing to invest in ourselves by *Commanding Respect*. But before we frantically turn to the pages of that section of HG21C, read on.

The main objective is to "selfishly" position ourselves so no one can question our intentions, resist our requests or wishes, - especially our wives. REPEAT

Though it's not an exact science, I can speak from my own experiences.

<u>Time + Effort = Giggles</u>

When I discovered the benefits and rewards for doing things that only took a few minutes or even a few seconds a day, I felt like I had discovered the "Source of the Nile".

(Please stop laughing, this is serious business.)

Let's take for example "one minute a day".

In only one minute we could:

1) Put the dishes in the dishwasher,
2) Rub her shoulders as we listen to the highlights of her day, or
3) Make up the bed.

We will be surprised at how sacrificing "one minute a day" will add to the "You owe me list".

Now try to imagine what we could do in only fifteen minutes a day.

1) Wash a load of laundry,
2) Dry a load of laundry (tomorrow),

3) Wash a car,
4) Mop the kitchen floor,
5) Vacuum the entire house,
6) Wash the dishes – by hand,
7) Give the kids and the dog a bath, then...

Watch the game or take a nap. The possibilities are endless.

Please understand – HG21C is not suggesting we go out and purchase a monogrammed apron with matching rubber gloves. - All we're doing is listing a few things that can be done in fifteen minutes.

Speaking of the *Household Chores and the Super Bowl.*

The Super Bowl Oath

We should always be able to sit comfortably in our dens and watch the game, - from the pre-game show to the post-game highlights, without being bothered by someone with "needs". And if sacrificing fifteen minutes a day will make the wife want to prepare sandwiches for my guests and then give me a "back and shoulder rub" during the halftime show – so be it.

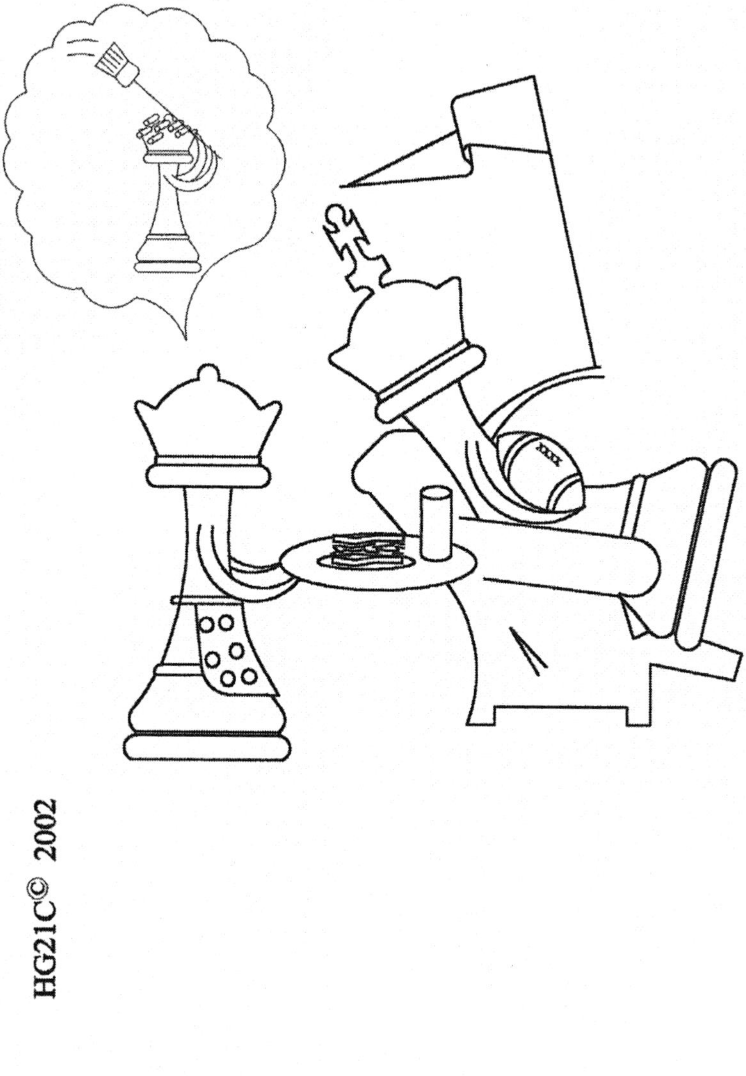
HG21C© 2002

Even if our wife is smarter than we are, she will have no other choice but to feel obligated to accommodate our wishes. Sure, one could argue this approach is manipulating or selfishly covert, but I prefer to look at it as War. And we all know that "All is Fair in Love and War".

HG21C Commercial Break

As we continue to read HG21C, every moment reading is a sacrifice of time that will reward us in the future. There are also many other "indirect rewards" to sacrificing our time - as discussed in *Making a Conscious Effort*.

OUR WIFE'S BEST FRIEND

Assuming that our wife is generally a happy person, we must accept the notion that her happiness is not based on *our* marriage relationship alone. There are many other elements in her life that contribute to her character and personality. Her best friend and relatives, for example, should especially be considered in this group.

Let's start by going back to the day's when we met our wife and eventually fell in love. Now asked, "What was it that made her so special"? Or perhaps, "Who" was it?

As we delve deeper into the influences that created our lovely maidens, we must also consider the city, neighborhood, and other environmental elements. Only then can we understand it wasn't just because she had a great pair of legs. And while we're at it, think of those elements that made "us" the man that we "were".

Fly on the Wall

In order to recognize the positive and negative elements of our marriage, we will need to look at "our position" from the outside – looking in. This will enable us to see the complete picture and also see where *we* fit in (?).

A good setting would be when we are in the company of our wife and one of her best girlfriends. If even for a few moments, pay close attention to how they react to each other.

Moreover, how does the girlfriend react to "you", and be aware and remember, if "girlfriend" is our wife's closest friend, chances are, whatever differences our wives and we have had over time, "girlfriend" has been briefed. Including the subject of *The Toilet Seat and Dirty Underwear.*

While we have every reason to believe that our marital issues and disagreements are private, "they" feel otherwise. This "security violation" is pretty much one of the basic characteristics of "women bonding". I personally believe that it's healthy, and besides, it has been going on for centuries. It's an Institution.

On the other hand, be advised - our wives have also briefed "girlfriend" on the positive things as well.

Issues: Out of Left-field

The problems usually occur on those occasions when our wives are not "completely satisfied" with how we verbally responded to them in a conversation – two weeks ago.

Though the real issue has nothing to do with two weeks ago, but is rather based on a "more recent" conversation with someone who falls into the category of *The Third Element*."

Having the position of being the wife's best friend is an extremely sensitive relationship. In some relationships, the girlfriend, (sister or mother) can have the kind of influence on our wives that promotes a balance of satisfaction and harmony.

There are many ways we could approach the girlfriend dilemma, but the safest is to be able to distinguish the good from the evil.

Type A

There's the Type A "girlfriend". You know, the one that reminds us of a bad movie. And from the moment she enters our home, we feel that it's a great time to clean our (nickel-plated) thirty-eight. Moreover, she always wants to remind us of the home improvement project that we never finished or perhaps the size of our behinds. But deep inside, we love her very much (?). And she loves us too (?). But don't fret.

Type A *could* be categorized as a favorable element in our lives. Not because of how "great" the two of us get along (?), but more of what the two of us [together] do for our wives. After all, our wife loves the both of us very much.

So put the thirty-eight away, girlfriend "A" is on our side.

<u>Type B</u>

The Type B girlfriend is the one that we really need to watch. They are usually the "miserably married", (or single), and have "issues" - all the damn time. Even our wife realizes she's an idiot, but for some reason, our wife feels that "girlfriend" can be helped (?). That's right, our wife is a part-time social worker.

On one hand, we should appreciate our wife's "willingness" to help the needy. On the other hand, girlfriend is trouble.

The reason(s) "B" is trouble is because she has the potential to negatively influence the harmony of our Empires, and more directly, our wives. My advice is to not even consider wasting a bullet.

Without completely minimizing the relationships between our wives and Needy-B, our problem is not really a problem, but a simple challenge.

If [you] we are searching for a way to completely rid ourselves of Needy B, there's a way we could [covertly] get our wife to do it.

A fair approach would be to refer to *Our Wife vs. Your Best Friend*. I am confident you can figure this one out. Besides a good assassin is hard to find these days.

The MOON, the STARS, and a ROCK

...No matter, we have decided to get married, and nothing can change our minds.

We walk out of the cinema holding hands, while sporting matching "outfits". She saves all of the ticket stubs and places them in a special box along with the rock we gave her on our first week [dating] anniversary.

We tell her that we will devote our lives, and will place the moon at her feet. We call her "Pookie"; she refers to [me] us as her "Sugar Bunny. And everyone say's, "We make a cute couple".

- Sorry to say, but becoming a newlywed negates all of the experiences referenced in the last two paragraphs. However, to succeed *will* require our best effort - still.

Accepting the fact that "life as we now know it", will no longer be the same and will completely transform overnight (?) - will require a great deal conviction and the desire to want to live "happily ever-after". Like in the movies?

Just "wanting" to become an HG21C member is not enough. Think about it. – Any membership that requires we first "Give Blood" - should give us "pause" to re-assess the situation. Then, we have to be trustworthy, loyal, helpful, friendly, courteous, kind, obedient, cheerful, brave, clean and reverent (?).

Moreover, we cannot afford to go into this venture without having the moon, the stars and all of the constellations in the proper alignment.

<u>Aligning the Stars</u>

Starting a new life "voluntarily" does not begin with just hiring the right wedding photographer or believing that she will accept another rock. We need to consider the environmental conditions as discussed in *Our Wife's Best Friend.*

Generally, a new environment has the ability to allow most of us to declare that we are "starting over", - a new life. We take with us the experiences of our youth, education and the influences of our environment and our families.

Hopefully, the experiences and influences we take with us are "only the better ones". And if we left a few of the better ones behind, let's go back and get them.

It is no different than when we begin a new job - in a new city, and then move into a new home, all within a matter of days. The change can either have many satisfying rewards or could become a complete disaster. So again, we cannot afford to leave home or move in - without [it] our best.

Promising the Moon

Promising Pookie the moon - to say the least, is "special". After all, the moon is up there just waiting to get plucked. Thus, the question is, "Is *that* what she wants"?

If she say's "Yes", the next question is, "Does she have somewhere to put it?

Okay, let's say Pookie *has* somewhere to put the moon. Now - all we have to do is put the moon in back of the rental truck, and hope to miss the rush hour traffic.

We slowly round the corner, back the truck into the driveway - slowly, and then roll the moon "uphill" into the house - where Pookie is waiting. She has chosen a special place in the living room, in the corner, - next to the sofa.

There it is, just like we promised, – we have placed the moon at her feet. - However…after a week, "POOKIE" discovered the moon did not match the drapes and *now* she wants the moon out of the house (?).

All together now…"@*# - $$$"

We argue that it would be "easier to just replace the "curtains", after all - we already returned the rental truck.

She responds, "@*# - NOW!"

(In other words, she resisted), and there we are, in rush hour traffic, slowly returning the moon.

Returning the Moon

As we sit there, with our right-turn-signal on, unable to see anything in our rearview mirrors, we ask ourselves, "How can we avoid this "@*# - situation" in the future"?

In the future - accept the fact, women and especially our wives are susceptible to "wanting things" and then returning them. The subject of shopping is one that HG21C cannot even begin to understand, let alone discuss. Forgive me.

It's no secret our economy is based on "wives buying stuff". Personally, my research shows marketing firms spend billions, on just marketing "my wife" alone. Pretty stiff competition – to say the least.

Since we have established *The Third Element,* we can now select the approach that will minimize the possibility of "it" ever happening again.

<u>Taking Notes</u>

The lesson learned from the "moon episode", was - we can now justify "questioning her judgment" in the future – but not out loud.

Understand, - she is fully aware that accepting the moon-gift was a mistake. Furthermore, she has convinced herself - the only reason she accepted the damn thing was because "we" wanted her to have it.

Her only concern at this point is hoping - "we don't question her judgment" – in the future.

Our next step is to (covertly) neutralize the opposition – but first, a little detour.

My Wife, or my Roommate?

Today, it's not much difference. Unless the kids have arrived, we basically live our lives as roommates. Especially when the both of us have full-time jobs. The only distinction in marriage is we have a common goal. – To be happy and prosper by making sound and logical decisions - together. The catch is, someone has to be "the thinker" all the time. In other words, "The both of us cannot afford to be stupid at the same time".

Summarizing the Moon issue

In the future, whenever a purchase involves renting a truck, along with a long-term financial commitment – think. "What's the sacrifice"? Then make certain everything matches.

For those of us who cannot *Understand What's Between These Lines,* - the moon *could* symbolize the fifty thousand dollar luxury SUV or the five-bedroom home that we promised her.

The moral of this story is to understand - the best decisions are made with honesty and *Logical Thinking.* -

Besides, it all started with a rock.

CONTINUE: FROM PAGE 3

Understand What's Between These Lines

...Therefore it is our responsibility to continue to grow intellectually, become less predictable and concentrate on bringing her back to the reality that first and foremost, she's our wife.

By all means, we must continue by *Making a Conscious Effort* to "impress the women" that will one day be asked to wipe the dribble from our mouths, change our bed pans or drive us to therapy.

<u>Clean the Mirror</u>

We can start by changing the source of our interests by engaging in alternative activities. In other words, make an effort to make ourselves more interesting instead of - what she *could* define as "predictable". Even if she does not say it out loud, a little "spontaneous change" would be, in the least - "fun".

Even if we have put on a few pounds, switching from boxers to briefs *may* at least make her giggle.

154 / HG21C

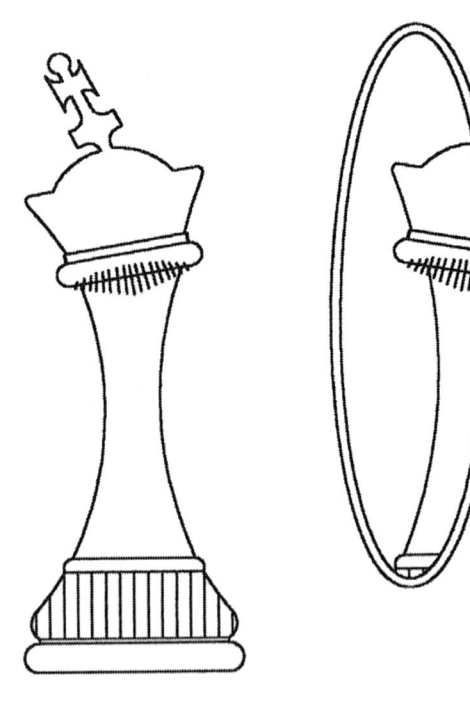

After all, making her "giggle" is what it's all about.

Now, Look in the Mirror

It has now been five, ten, fifteen or 20 YEARS, and somehow we believe that our wives *should* still find us attractive? Sure, she's put on a couple of pounds as well, but if she got rid of those flannel pajamas, life would be a little bit better.

Many of us have always had our own style with regard to the way we dress, the style of our hair, clean-shaven, with or without a beard. We chose this "look" because at one time it captured the attention of that girl that eventually became our wife. And maybe…it's time for a change.

Growing, or getting rid of the beard – *temporarily,* would certainly allow her to experience a taste of "variety". We could also replace our multi-purpose sweat pants with black satin loungewear. And as we throw out the sweat pants, we might as well declare her flannel pajamas as "missing in action".

Old Dog – Same Tricks

If one of our predictable habits, while driving, is listening to the same music radio station, we *could* alternate by listening to talk radio. Even if we do not agree with the subject matter, the information will provide us with a bit of insight into "worldly affairs", which could come in handy during casual conversations with Mrs. Know-it-all or *The Telephone Queen.*

Some of us make the mistake by acquiring an interest in activities that are self-indulging, such as playing 18 holes or by pampering a new car – just to get out of the house. These are simple hobbies that – if abused, could minimize our growth as individuals and ignore the issues at hand.

This is easy for me to say, - I drive a pickup and have never broken 100.

HG21C / 157

HG21C© 2002

SUMMARIZING HG21C

It is no mistake - I chose "not" to list this summary in the *Table of Contents,* because it is important we read and understand HG21C in its entirety before we review.

HG21C was written for the husband that is searching for answers and sincerely "wants" to make his marriage work – by any means necessary. With this said…

It is sincerely my hope that we can clearly see – "what we are up against" and what efforts we need to take in order to transform that "woman" into the kind of wife we long for.

"This is not a short course" by any means.

Defining the Dilemma

If you recall, we are faced with accepting the fact that there is no "established definition" of the term *Wife*.

As startling as this discovery may be, it really allows our wives to "choose what kind of wife – she wants be". And how she makes this choice will depend on "how we express our expectations". It is also extremely important that before we approach her with our list of "wants" we must first position ourselves to avoid her "What about me"(?) defense.

Making a Conscious Effort

Remember, this one is – **TOP SECRET.**

This chapter discusses the notion of "evaluating ourselves" – as *Husbands*. It also references by "what standards" do we adopt (?).

If we review the definition of *Husband,* it is our responsibility to be the "Master of the household" whether we like it or not.

This responsibility has absolutely nothing to do with challenging our wives as being equal partners, but rather – recognizing that managing the household not only involves keeping the home safe and secure, but also includes contributing to the household chores. REPEAT

Managing the home is serious business and is no way a trend. After all, our responsibilities as *Husbands* "are clearly defined". Moreover, we cannot truly "take command" - unless we approach our responsibility with fair decisions and *Logical Thinking.*

Logical Thinking

Simply, we must always be able to acknowledge the negative "influences" in order to address or to completely eliminate the "matters at hand".

As we discussed in *Pleading Guilty,* we can feel confident that when she "questions our intentions", it is usually inspired by a *Third Element.*

This chapter also acknowledged that our most important responsibility is to be her "hero" - which could be as simple as sacrificing a little time - listening.

The Third Element

This chapter discusses - acknowledging "what *Elements"* are causing the static or the disagreements, and to accept the responsibility to eliminate them. We must also be able to accept the notion that the *Movement* is our biggest challenge.

A Distant Third Place

I will admit - this chapter is one of my favorites.

To acknowledge, "When a wife becomes a mother, – she becomes ninety-nine percent mother" is one of the basic foundations of our dilemma.

Additionally, our actions and decisions must be based on the reality that – until the kids are gone, we have no reason to expect to be "her first priority". – Unless we are a Super Husband.

We must also be sincerely appreciative and completely supportive of the responsibilities that our wives feel dedicated to undertake.

The Power of the Movement

Let's be careful with this one - by quietly acknowledging - the [Women's] *Movement's* agenda does not benefit *Husbands,* but rather places us in the general category of men. We must also remember…

She has accepted the notion that "representing the *Movement"* is a full-time responsibility, which conflicts with the idea of being "wifely".

With this said…

Our first objective with regard to the *Movement* is to completely support our wives in their quest to fulfill their career aspirations as "women in the workplace" – period.

Our second objective is to respectfully communicate to our wives that – when she is at home, she should be completely comfortable with letting her hair down and "being a girl" – giggles and all.

Understand(ing) What's Between These Lines

I will admit, as this chapter was being written, I had no idea what the title would be. For example, if you were to review the first three paragraphs of this chapter, I am certain that you recall "the first reading - required re-reading" in order to understand - what took me a week and a half to write.

The main objective of this chapter was for [us] to acknowledge that we yearn for our wives to display their "feminine charms", and to also find a legitimate way to get rid of her flannel pajamas.

Commanding Respect

Imagine George Washington crossing the Delaware River – standing at the helm, proudly representing a successful Revolution and the Birth of our Nation.

Now imagine George standing at the helm while the entire crew had the opinion that he was a complete idiot (?).

When Decisions Become Regrets

If you recall, this chapter discussed decisions that could become "life-long regrets". It also mentioned the "landmines in high-heel shoes".

I realized this topic is one of the most sensitive chapters of HG21C – but is also the reason why some of our brothers are sporting orange jumpsuits - while waiting to be arraigned.

While *we* cannot judge whether or not they are guilty, they will be arraigned as soon as their attorney finishes up a racketeering case, involving a guy who was charged with soliciting two five-year-olds (hit-girls) in the schoolyard.

Sacrificing Time

All right, I will admit - it takes longer than fifteen minutes to wash a car – Forgive me.

What this chapter is attempting to communicate is "our wives" cannot hold a full-time job, take care of the kids, perform the household chores - by her self, and then have the energy to concentrate on being "wifely".

Remember, "our lack of support" in contributing to the household chores is what most of our wives complained about most – and rightly so. We must remember the 15-minute sacrifice and the *Super Bowl Oath?*

The Moon, the Stars and a Rock

I will start by *Pleading Guilty* – this chapter was a last minute addition.

As a veteran *Husband,* my main objective in writing HG21C was to address the concerns of my fellow veterans. However, we cannot afford to leave the *Newlyweds* out of the picture for the mere reason – we need to recognize them as our protégés.

Imagine our reaction when "Grasshopper" announces - he is engaged and will be "tying the knot" in June. - Don't laugh – he's "in love".

Just congratulate him, and as a wedding gift, we wrap up a copy of HG21C.

Now we can laugh.

HG21C / 167

The HG21C Cast

AUTHOR'S ANNOUNCEMENT:

While this edition of HG21C has covered many important topics – such as *Defining the Dilemma,* I am excited to announce the second edition of HG21C is on the way and will be available Spring 2003.

HG21C©
"Husband's Guide to the 21st Century"

"Chapter Five"
By: M. Anthony Bell

HG21C Chapter Five © will cover the topics we could not discuss in the first edition of HG21C. - I am sure you will understand. And yes, *Chapter Five* will include "*that*" subject.

.

Final Note: To the Wives

Please imagine [yourselves] sitting in a very large chair adorned with precious stones and trimmed in gold. Your posture is "straight" as your elbows rest on the arms of your ornamented thrown, while your hands sit-folded in your lap. Beautiful...

NOW imagine me standing before you in a nice suit (that I purchased myself). Standing behind me are millions of other husbands - also wearing nice suits. But, we have on the tie you purchased on our last birthday. - We look good too.

Though we could not afford to purchase a million roses for our lapels, we stand before you with the hope that we have respectfully presented our dilemma.

Please remember, we are not as complicated or as lazy as we appear. We just require the motivation that can only be inspired by your feminine charms.

HG21C© 2002

ISBN 155369648-4

9 781553 696483

Made in the USA